Paul Binding was born in 1943, [...]
Germany and the north of Englan[...]
hamsted School and New College[...]
teacher and a university lecturer, and on the staff of the *New
Statesman*. From 1985–86 he was the Eudora Welty Visiting
Professor at Millsaps College, Jackson, Mississippi. He is the
author of *Separate Country: a Literary Journey through the
American South* and *Lorca: the Gay Imagination*; two novels,
*Harmonica's Bridegroom* and *Kingfisher Weather*; and a volume of
poetry with John Horder, *Dreams and Speculations*. A study of
Eudora Welty will be published shortly. He writes regularly on
animal rights matters as well as on literature.

and after a childhood in
and was educated at Berk-
Oxford. He has been a

PAUL BINDING

# St Martin's Ride

PICADOR
Published by Pan Books

First published 1990 by Martin Secker & Warburg Ltd
This revised Picador edition with a new afterword
first published 1992 by Pan Books Ltd,
Cavaye Place, London SW10 9PG
1 3 5 7 9 8 6 4 2
© Paul Binding 1990, 1992
ISBN 0 330 32359 8

Grateful acknowledgement is made to the following for permission to quote copyright
material: Thames & Hudson Ltd for *The Expressionists* by Wolf-Dieter Dube, p. 117; Anvil
Press Poetry for *Poems of Paul Celan*, p. 132; Edward Arnold for *Howard's End* by
E. M. Forster, p. 121.

Printed in England by Clays Ltd, St Ives plc

For Mark Todd

I must thank Tom Rosenthal, then of Secker and Warburg, for having the faith in this project to commission it. I would also like to thank Dan Franklin and Vicky Harris now at Secker and Warburg for their help.

The Goethe Institute, the cultural wing of the embassy of the Federal German Republic, was generous enough to give me a grant for travelling in Germany. The Phoenix Trust of London, too, kindly provided financial assistance for my researches.

Peter Graves of the German department of the University of Leicester took time and trouble to supervise the German for this edition. I am very grateful indeed to him.

Outside official institutions, so many people have been helpful to me that it is impossible to thank them all in such a short space. But I would like to acknowledge here my gratitude to the following: Johannes Balwe; David Fernbach; Michael Fischer; Francesca Goddard; Nic Hill; Claire Hiscock; Wim Hottentot; Antonia Inlander; Isolde Kauffmann; the staff of Mount Pleasant; Sara Parkin; Frans de Rover; John Saumarez Smith; Norbert and Jutta Schumann; Mark Todd; Christopher and Helen Watkins; and Martin Fletcher at Picador.

PART ONE

# Essen

# One

In a suburban house in Germany a little boy stands by an upstairs window, intent on the dark, silent street below. Any minute now, St Martin will appear, wearing only half a cloak and riding a white horse. The other half of his cloak he has given away to a beggar. It's the eve of the saint's own day, 11 November, when, every year, he rides through the city followed by the young. But in fact these last years this ride of his hasn't been possible. 'Why not?' the boy, suspecting the terrible truth, asks the two women on either side of him – Toni, plump, dough-faced, comfortable; Trude, thin, sharp-featured, bright-eyed. They don't answer, but he hasn't really expected them to. Presently Toni holds up a hand. 'Listen,' she says, 'and watch.' The song that has been faintly audible for some while all of a sudden swells. St Martin is turning into Tirpitzstraße itself, and behind him comes his retinue.

Toni and Trude, the boy realises, are as excited as he is, perhaps more so, because, after all, they've seen St Martin and his troupe before. Jesus Christ, they've told him, was so pleased with St Martin that he appeared to him in a

3

dream, dressed in the very half-cloak the saint gave to the beggar.

The remaining half of the cloak is visible now, a shining white, more discernible at first than its wearer or his white mount. St Martin's deed was not just kind, thinks the boy, but extremely brave, for the night is very cold. Everyone has been saying that winter has already arrived, and Toni even has a song about it:

> A, a, a, der Winter, der ist da.
> Herbst und Sommer sind vergangen,
> Winter, der hat angefangen.
> A, a, a, der Winter, der ist da!

(A, a, a, winter is here. Autumn and summer are past, winter has begun. A, a, a, winter is here!)

And everyone is saying too that the winter ahead will be a hard one.

But where is the beggar now? the boy wonders. Probably asleep, the half-cloak wrapped as tightly as possible round him, on one of the city's many thousand piles of rubble, most of which are covered with frost.

The horse is old, St Martin is youthful, his followers are younger still. Their song flows down tree-lined Tirpitzstraße like an undammed stream. All the children singing it are holding up lanterns, head-high or higher, and what lanterns too! Just as the boy has never seen so many children all together at the same time, so he has never imagined that lanterns could take such various forms: castles, candles, cathedrals, animals, birds, fishes, cheerful faces, grotesque

4

faces, scarcely human faces. The light they shed on Tirpitz-straße is a wonderful blend of red, green, purple, silver, gold. Now St Martin is clopping slowly past the boy's home – No. 49 – and the children become more distinguishable. They look proud and solemn. But then the beauty of their lanterns is reason enough for pride, and what they're hon-ouring is something very solemn. The carol, as it swirls in this stretch of the street, brings St Martin face to face again with his beggar:

> *Im Schnee, da saß ein armer Mann,*
> *hatt' Kleider nicht, hatt' Lumpen an.*
> *O helft mir doch in meiner Not,*
> *sonst ist der bittre Frost mein Tod!*

(In the snow there sat a poor man, he had no clothes, he had only tatters on. O help me now in my need, otherwise the bitter frost is my death!)

Toni and Trude keep glancing at the boy, and he under-stands that his pleasure pleases them. It's pleasure tinged with envy, for he would like to be down there among the lantern-bearers himself. Like Toni's Hannelore and Trude's Günter, both of whom they now try to spot.

The boy thinks: this procession should go on for ever, and the lanterns should never cease to shine before my house. He won't leave the window until the children have become invisible again and the song faint.

If St Martin were to meet another beggar, would he give him the half-cloak he's retained? But if he did, the saint himself would die, and all his many young followers would

5

be let down. And, another question: where will all of these go to when the celebrations have come to an end? The boy sees few children who don't live in the same street as himself, and all of those are – like himself – English.

Beyond the suburb where stands his house lies a city that is a desert, a region not of presences but of absences.

When he gets into bed that night, he thinks about Hannelore and Günter. Hannelore has long, fair plaits; she's good at skipping and at pushing him on his swing so that he can fly upwards into the tree's own world of sky-patterning branches. She's taught him some pretty songs: '*Kommt ein Vogel geflogen*', for instance, and '*Es klappert die Mühle*':

> *Es klappert die Mühle am rauschenden Bach,*
> *klipp, klapp.*
> *Bei Tag und bei Nacht ist der Müller stets wach,*
> *klipp, klapp!*
> *Er mahlet das Korn zu dem täglichen Brot,*
> *und haben wir, dieses, so hat's keine Not.*
> *Klipp, klapp, klipp, klapp, klipp, klapp! (bis)*

(The mill clatters round by the rushing stream, clip-clap. By day and by night the miller is always awake, clip-clap! He grinds the corn for the daily bread, and if we have this, then we're not hungry. Clip-clap, clip-clap, clip-clap.)

The chorus, as Hannelore sings it, imitates first the rotation and then the slowing-down of the mill-wheel and the boy always sees before him that mill at the end of one of the walks his mother and he regularly take – set by a stream

6

(though it does not rush along) and with a great wheel (though this is still and slime-covered). But maybe one day it will be working again. 'Things,' he hears so often, 'will *eventually* get back to normal.'

His favourite song of all, however, is one which – for all the exuberance of its nonsensical refrain – has a sadness he is never sure he can bear:

> *Auf einem Baum ein Kuckuck,*
> *simsaladim, bamba, saladu, saladim,*
> *auf einem Baum ein Kuckuck saß.*

(On a tree, a cuckoo, simsaladim, bamba, saladu, saladim, on a tree a cuckoo sat.)

But not for long. A hunter came and shot the cuckoo, shot him dead as the last line, the last *word* of the verse, makes inescapably plain. But then things were put right – or so it would seem:

> *Und als ein Jahr vergangen,*
> *simsaladim, bamba, saladu, saladim,*
> *und als ein Jahr vergangen war,*

> *da war der Kuckuck wieder,*
> *simsaladim, bamba, saladu, saladim,*
> *da war der Kuckuck wieder da.*

(And when a year had gone by, there was the cuckoo back again.)

How? *How* had it defied death? Was that how the world

7

worked? Would all those who'd died in this city – during those years when St Martin was unable to ride through it – come back one day?

Trude's Günter is about the same age as Hannelore (eleven, twelve), a lively, stocky boy, invariably dressed in much-patched shorts. He is very keen on football – and the boy himself has requested a football as his Christmas present. Günter too knows many songs, and has a sweet, true voice, which he is not shy of using.

Once the two of them, Günter and he, were in the dining-room by themselves. The table was laid for dinner. Günter, with a saucy, inclusive smile, nudged him and said: '*Wir sind böse Männer.*' ('We're bad men.') He then started picking things up from the table – a knife, a spoon, some nuts – and stuffing them into his pockets or up his jersey. The boy was not shocked but fascinated. In fact he almost admired Günter for what seemed like a challenge to just about everything. Anyway, Günter later put all the things back.

Another occupation delights Günter every bit as much as football – playing the harmonica. He is rarely without this instrument. He's always able to coax melodies from it which spread themselves upon the air like some bright banner made of sound. Günter's entire face emanates joy when he moves the harmonica across his mouth and works its stops. Some of the tunes he makes up (or so he says), others are those of the songs that have already become such a part of the boy's own life here.

He doesn't know where Hannelore and Günter live. Not with their mothers anyway, who have a room each at the top of Tirpitzstraße 49. And certainly not with their fathers.

8

Toni's husband and Trude's husband are – both of them – missing in Russia. These very words alarm the boy who sees the two men stumbling, frantic but exhausted, about a huge, treeless plain such as he's been told Russia consists of. Toni and Trude both say their men will never leave Russia alive. In private the boy's parents say that they're probably right to suppose this. They talk quite a bit about Russia themselves. What is it going to do? In particular, what is it going to do in the most important city in the country – Berlin?

Whatever Russia does or doesn't do, the boy thinks, nothing worse can happen than has already happened here. Could anything match in awfulness what accosts you when you leave this suburb of Bredeney and enter the city proper, the city called Essen?


And even Bredeney itself isn't entirely free from sights to make you shudder.

One day his mother decided on a new route for one of their twice-daily walks. (She's spent most of her life in the country, and is restless in the town, even in a district like Bredeney, whose roads are all planted with trees, which is full of gardens and little woods, and has a lake of its own, the Balderneysee.) Weekday walks are safe, as weekend drives are not. But this one . . .

They were not going to the place where his father worked, the Villa Hügel, by the beech-wooded ravine, their usual route. They were making their way there along a different wood-path. Which turned abruptly, and, without warning, showed him what he dreaded most to see. There a row of

9

them stood, a row of those dreadful battered houses: roofless, the walls jagged-edged at the top, fractured and burned shells that contained (or just about contained, for often it spilled out) a senseless mess of stones and metal.

They heralded others of their kind beyond counting. Whatever had brought it all about? Whatever was it that had struck here, even in pleasant-seeming Bredeney, as it had, so much more extensively, in Essen itself?

Nobody has been able to explain things.


He hasn't always lived in Germany. But, except when prompted by his mother, he doesn't remember England well, just certain barely connectable objects, moments, scenes, which he can shake about in his head like a kaleidoscope. His mother and himself playing with a quoit in their small back garden. A ginger cat called Peter. Blinds that you pulled down every night for the 'black-out'. A friend of his parents who cracked plum-stones with her teeth but told him not to imitate her. A Mickey Mouse gas mask. Walks up a wide, grass-verged street into the village. A café there with a beamed ceiling, and people making a fuss of him, and delicious cakes. Getting to know his two favourite books, *The Tale of Peter Rabbit* (with its picture of the rabbit hiding in a watering-can, two ears protruding however), and *The Tale of Tom Kitten* (with its equally delightful picture of the kittens being wildly naughty up in the bedroom). The village was Broadway, Worcestershire. Sometimes they left Broadway for Bideford in Devon, where his grandparents lived. Occasionally, here in Germany, his father tells him about his grandfather who is now dead. He'd been a clergyman, a man of God, and the boy looks a bit like him, he's told, and has the same wart on the back of his head. Possibly he might grow up to be a clergyman himself.

In England, too, he learned his favourite song – apart, that is, from *'Es klappert die Mühle'* and *'Auf einem Baum'*:

> Upon Paul's steeple stands a tree
> As full of apples as can be;
> The little boys of London Town
> They run with sticks to fetch them down.
> And then they run from hedge to hedge
> Until they come to London Bridge.

Perhaps he likes the song because it has his own name in it. But he likes it even more because of the captivating picture it paints. On a spire there grows a fruit-laden tree, yet not so high up that the boys cannot get at the apples. And boys can run together through fields, it would seem, until they reach London Bridge. He imagines Günter of their number, perhaps even kicking his football as he goes along.

They changed trains in London when bound for Germany, but he's never properly seen it. Whenever he tries to envisage it, it turns into the emptiness of Essen. Anyway, his parents talk less about London now than they do about Berlin – which is, they say, in an even sorrier state than the city close by their house.

His father explained to him in England that they were moving to Germany because it was a duty to help that country as much as you could. Whatever anyone else said, he

**11**

must never forget that the Germans were a great, a wonderful people. The boy's father spoke German perfectly, his mother had already learned some, and he himself would be speaking German before very long.

His father left for Germany in advance of his mother and himself. Their own journey there differed in his mind from the English life they said goodbye to because he could recollect it sequentially, not just in fragments.

They got on to the boat at Tilbury for the voyage which lasted three full days, far longer than it once took, he was told, because the North Sea was still not clear of mines. (Mines could explode and destroy the ship even so far from land.) The sea was rough, but he loved the fierce play of the waves, and his mother said that this was because he came, on her side, from an old seafaring family. Out in the middle of the sea there were no birds; these came again, swooping, calling, beckoning, with the low, green, German coast.

All the passengers disembarked at Cuxhaven, and there he was taken to a hotel where he saw with amazement a totally new kind of lavatory, a German kind, which showed you what you'd done on a gleaming shelf, before flushing it away. Then followed the train journey made by night. Everything was organised by the British Army, who issued a complete batch of different numbered and coloured tickets and advised people to listen carefully at stations for instructions relayed from loudspeakers.

His mother explained that from now on the Army would be very important in their lives: they were running this part of Germany. But he mustn't think his father was in the Army, he would not be pleased; he had hoped for other arrangements for the German people than military occupation. His father was a civilian: an accountant, an economist. His parents had not been separated during the war, his father having had a 'reserved occupation', and they'd lived together in Broadway for almost its entire duration.

The train travelled through a dark, all-but-invisible Germany; the carriages were continually shunted about, information was continually blared out into the night at virtually lightless stations. Between the messages music was played to keep everyone cheerful, awake, alert; his mother said she would never want to hear the 'Skaters' Waltz' or the 'Blue Danube Waltz' again.

Had he been physically unable to move from his place in the railway compartment or had he just been dozy through travel-weariness? Whatever the reasons, he was utterly unprepared for what Essen presented to him.

There on the platform was standing his father and, at his side, an older man with a weather-beaten face. He was introduced as Stumpfer, their driver. The boy had rarely been in a car before; it was exciting climbing into it, knowing that he was about to see a new place (a city!) and a new home. The car left the station yard . . .

And now the past becomes the present, and that dreadful moment of confrontation is with him again, a moment in which the whole world was revealed as other than he'd ever thought – or even feared. The *broken buildings* are thrust on him, as in some huge obscene joke.

He covers his eyes with his hands. What he's seen can't be true! He removes his hands, but there they are still, not the same ruins, but others – with yet more in sight, waiting

13

to show their ghastly forms. He screams. There seems no other way for him to express the feelings they instantly inspire.

Screaming does not make the ruins go away.

His father said to his mother: 'The damage here is very bad. I don't think people back in England realise just how bad it really is.'

Damage: you used that word for a toy, a piece of furniture, something in the post. Not for a town, a place where people live. (But then *did* people live here? *Could* they do so? There was nobody about.)

His father said that Toni (cook) and Trude (housekeeper) were greatly looking forward to their first meeting with him. The boy must appear pleased to be in Germany.

Very soon it had come to seem that he'd lived nowhere else. But he could remember his relief when he'd found an end to broken buildings: their house stood in a very solid, almost cheerful street. Toni and Trude he took to at once: they shook him by the hand, which was strange. No one had ever shaken him by the hand before, though now it's something he expects: after all Toni does it every morning when she brings him his mug of hot chocolate.

It is curious to think that when he arrived at Tirpitzstraße 49 he was unable to understand what Toni, Trude and Stumpfer were saying. Now it's as if their language just *happened* to him – like the weather. Not to know German, not to have two languages to choose from, was not to be himself.

But he knows how he felt as he witnessed his father talking away in German and then interpreting replies to his mother and himself: the boy understood at once that his father had changed, that he was not the man he'd known before in Broadway.

'Toni and Trude say,' his father tells him, 'you could be a German child with your fair hair and your blue eyes – and the kind of stocky build you have . . .'


If he did look like a German child, he could have slipped into the Martinmas procession without being noticed. He could go home to parents he'd call Mutti and Vati, which were sometimes how his father referred to Mummy and himself. His father believed that they should speak German, even in the house, as much as possible. It was extremely bad manners, not to say hurtful, to be speaking English when Toni and Trude were around. What would they think?

The house itself is a pleasant place, large though semi-detached. Its front wall is covered in creeper, there are three storeys and a basement. A balcony runs the length of it, overlooking the well-stocked garden. On the lawn there grows a magnolia-tree; his mother had been very pleased when she'd found this: she'd always, it had turned out, wanted one.

Sometimes in the comfort of the centrally-heated house or enjoying the delights of the garden (out of sight of old Peter, the gardener, who occasionally decides to sleep down in the basement), you can feel that you've made up the broken buildings and all those silences that fill them, all those silences that wash their inhospitable exteriors.

*

Every day now is colder than its predecessor. It's evening, and there comes a ring at the door. Who on earth can it be? Toni doesn't appear to have heard the bell, so the boy's mother goes to answer it. Soon he can hear her talking in her fast but flustered German. He goes into the hall and sees, framed in the doorway, three children. They are somewhat older than himself, the age of the children in the St Martin's Eve procession.

There are two boys and a girl. In the arms of one of the boys is a small black dog.

No beguiling lantern lights up these children's faces now, though. The harsh electricity of the hall shows them as thin, hollow-cheeked, determined-eyed. Their clothes are ill-fitting, and the boys wear trousers far more patched than Günter's. There is an intensity in these children's manner that is disconcerting; certainly it disconcerts his mother, who will, the boy feels sure, break down when they have gone and say what a dreadful, dreadful place this Germany is. But now she is explaining to him what the children were suggesting before he appeared: they can no longer look after their little dog, they haven't enough to eat themselves. They're offering him in exchange for some food.

Of course the boy knows his mother will agree. Not only is she very fond of children (of Hannelore and Günter, for instance), she is very fond of animals too. As for himself, he has been wanting a dog for, it now seems, a long time.

The dog is a skeleton loosely clad in a shaggy black coat. His eyes are sad and uncomprehending. His whole being is like a plea, one that knows it's unlikely to be answered. The boy's mother goes into the kitchen and comes out with some

**16**

bread, and with biscuits, chocolate, cocoa and a tin of powdered milk. The children thank the Englishwoman in that ritualistic manner almost all German children have, and which he – thanks to Toni and Trude – is himself beginning to acquire. They don't show pleasure or gratitude, even though they've probably got far more food than they'd expected. Necessary business has been done.

'What's the dog's name?' asks his mother.

'Debs,' the children say in chorus, 'his name is Debs.'

And Debs is formally handed over. The bargain has been concluded. But as the trio moves out through the door, back into the bitter night, the boy who'd been holding the dog turns round to look at it – already another's. Tears are rolling down his face. Pride and sorrow make him shuffle quickly on, and he vanishes with his companions. To go where?

The boy must learn how to look after Debs, who will sleep downstairs in the *Wintergarten*. This is a room the like of which he hadn't encountered in England but which he sees regularly enough here in Essen. All four walls of this room – which has one door into the dining-room and another on to the terrace – are of glass, which makes it a fine place to be now that winter is arriving. His father says that Germans have a respect for the sun, a sensible attitude towards its properties, that no other people possess. Their houses show this.

So Debs sleeps in a warm room among plants and between the basket chairs.

It soon seems as if Debs has been with them always. He

**17**

accompanies the boy and his mother on all their walks. Many afternoons they make their way to the Villa Hügel to meet his father when his day's work is over.

The Villa Hügel must be the vastest, the most impressive building in the whole world. Behind it landscaped gardens descend to the shores of the Balderneysee. Its entrance hall could itself contain many a house, and in it the British of the area, of the Occupation, can exchange greetings. It is hung with huge paintings of stern, grand-looking people framed in thick gold against any possibility of ordinariness. Leading off the hall is a dining-room with a table stretching almost into invisibility, and glinting with silver and glass. Here, apparently, the family who owned the Villa until just over a year ago entertained monarchs, princes, heads of state. The boy imagines men and women wearing crowns and scarlet robes sitting themselves down as trumpets fanfared. The members of this family must have been like monarchs themselves. Their name was Krupp, and the organisation his father works for is usually referred to as Krupp's, though in fact it belongs to the British Coal Board. Where are the family now? Not in Essen, certainly. When the name of its head, Alfred Krupp, is mentioned, faces and voices change. The boy finds extraordinary the widespread, grim interest in Alfred's present whereabouts. When he asks, the answer comes very reluctantly – and not from his parents, but from Geoffrey, the Englishman who lives next door and who also has an office in the Villa Hügel. Alfred Krupp is in prison.

The very word is chilling. The boy thinks first of all of the washroom in the basement of Tirpitzstraße 49, where he was once accidentally shut in. But that had not been a frightening room, except that you couldn't get out of it; maybe Alfred was somewhere more like those cellars which he knew to lie, unreachably, far beneath the city's interminable rubble. Alfred's imprisonment is something (though what?) to do with a town called Nuremburg. Nuremburg was not a name he liked to hear because – even over the dining-table, or in the ease of the drawing-room – it was a signal for the disagreements between his parents that took place ever more frequently.

His mother would say that she would like to go to Nuremburg, it would be interesting, it was history in the making. Lots of English people, many whom she knows, have been and returned impressed.

His father would bat his eyelids at this point, which meant that he was also batting back real anger. (He was someone who never shouted or lost his temper.) He found it completely disgusting, he said, that people went to a trial as if it were a public entertainment. It was medieval. Didn't his mother understand that being condemned to death there meant that real people were to be killed? What kind of civilisation did we have if we gloated over deaths of members of a government?

'*Members of a government!*' his mother exclaims, 'is that what you call them?'

'They *were* members of a government whether we like it or not. I don't see how one could deny the fact,' says his father. 'And I don't approve of *anybody* being hanged.'

The boy has glimpsed a picture of a hanging in a history book his mother is keeping for him when he is older. How could a man with a palatial house of his own and estate-like gardens with terraces and grottoes, with princes as friends and ancestors austerely larger than life between gold frames, be strung up from a rope?

Another saint will visit Essen, but he won't make a public appearance like St Martin. This is St Nicholas, the children's very own saint, whose yearly visit (on the eve of 6 December) is made expressly for their sake, to please them with presents.

There's a rousing song heralding him:

> *Niklaus, komm in unser Haus,*
> *pack die großen Taschen aus.*
> *Lustig, lustig, traleralala,*
> *bald ist Niklausabend da,*
> *bald ist Niklausabend da!*

(Nicholas, come to our house, empty out your big bags. Joyful, joyful, traleralala, St Nicholas's Eve is soon here!)

The next verses are very intriguing, making you tingle for the night to arrive:

> *Stell das Pferdchen untern Tisch,*
> *daß es Heu und Hafer frißt.*
> *Lustig, lustig . . .*

> *Heu und Hafer frißt es nicht,*
> *Zuckerplätzchen kriegt es nicht.*
> *Lustig, lustig . . .*

(Put the little horse under the table, so that it eats hay and oats. Joyful, joyful . . . Hay and oats it doesn't eat, little plates of sweetmeats it won't get. Joyful, joyful . . .)

When the saucers are placed under the table, as the song commands, what will St Nicholas do? In the morning the boy finds all three of them filled with nuts, sultanas and raisins – one for himself, one for Hannelore, one for Günter.

When you went to bed at night, it was best to try to concentrate on such people as St Martin or St Nicholas – or to think of Debs, for that matter. But, even so, wicked visitations could take place in his sleep. Sometimes the very centre of Essen seemed to be trying to establish itself in his own head.

His is a nice room, with a rose-patterned wallpaper and french windows opening on to the balcony. Round his bed he's ranged his toy animals as a guard – an elephant, a kangaroo, a tiger, a rabbit, a bear.

One thing he is absolutely sure of: those buildings were broken for no good purpose at all. If an object smashes, then you try to mend it; but there can be no easy mending here in Germany. The smashing has been too thorough, the houses ground down as by a cruel and incalculably vast boot. And the people that were inside them?

At first it seems as if *this* street is going to be all right. Three children have beckoned him along it. Are they the ones who brought Debs to the door? Perhaps they're wanting the dog back?

Nevertheless he follows them. It's dark, just as in the real world beyond his sleep. At the end of the street looms a huge church. When he arrives in the square where it stands, he is alone. The mighty façade rearing up before him seemed, at a casual glance, intact, but now he can see there's a fissure in it, and the fissure is widening. Some malevolent act has been planned. Very soon the fissure will have widened so much that the whole edifice will come crashing down on him. It'll leave hillocks of stone and scorched brick, and he himself will lie buried underneath.

That *is* what happened to many people in Essen, including children such as himself, isn't it?

Yes, it's falling now, and with a slow inevitability – because all the churches he's ever seen in cities have been broken. Why should this one be any exception? Even so he can't help crying out, in fright, in protest.

And now he can feel, not tumbling stones, but his counterpane and the soft contours of the toy animals that rest on it. And his mother has appeared. It takes him a few minutes, though, to stop screaming, as if there's a part of that descending church inside his skull which is *outside* it, threatening him with its debris. A little reluctantly his mother says he'd better come downstairs for a while. From the drawing-room the familiar sounds of the grand piano are drifting up. His father is having a lesson from Dr Ahlens. The boy puts on his scarlet dressing-gown and follows his mother into the drawing-room.

Dr Ahlens is tall, silver-haired, a little stooping, more like a stork than a man, and surely very ancient. He comes to the house three times a week; he and the boy's father are working their way through the *Zweistimmige Inventionen* of J. S. Bach. They pause when the boy comes into the room; he can see that his father is not at all pleased by his appearance. These lessons are of the greatest importance to him.

'*So*,' says Dr Ahlens, 'the child is upset again; *der arme Paul*, never mind, his trouble will pass, troubles do eventually.'

Mysterious words of his parents about Dr Ahlens come back: 'I'm quite sure he knew nothing about *any* of it. I mean, he's such a good man. He just lives for music and for teaching it to others. I doubt . . . I doubt if he'd ever so much as *heard* of the man.'

What could the 'it' be? Who was 'the man'?

Dr Ahlens is now addressing himself to a fingering problem of his father's . . .

'What is it, Paul?'

His mother is asking him this. She knows that though his nightmare has left him exhausted, he is possessed by a question he has to articulate.

'*Who* damaged Essen – and all the other cities?'

Of course he knows by now there'll be no answer. His father and Dr Ahlens exchange pitying, concerned glances. Then their music begins again, four hands asking questions of each other, receiving answers, agreeing with each other, then debating anew . . . It could go on for ever, you feel. Though the boy prefers '*Kommt ein Vogel geflogen*' and '*Ich habe mein Herz in Heidelberg verloren*', he finds a restful fascination in this piece. He follows its dialogue until he has fallen asleep again, when his mother carries him back upstairs.

Where does Dr Ahlens live? Oh, in a room somewhere out in the city. We're not sure exactly. He's too proud to tell us about it.

On his next visit Dr Ahlens arrives with a large box. He was very sorry, he says, to see *der kleine Paul* so upset; he can remember only too well bad dreams from his own boyhood. So here is a present, something he himself had in his long-ago childhood. With protestations, and then with effusive thanks, the box is accepted.

It turns out to contain a toy village, or rather the components of a village that can be arranged – and rearranged – in any order and to make a place of any shape you want. There are steep-roofed houses, there's a church with a slender, red-spired tower, there's a bridge, there are bigger buildings clearly mayorial, and – possibly the best of the lot – there's a water-mill with a wheel that turns. '*Es klappert die Mühle am rauschenden Bach*'. There's no doubt that it's a German village. He's glimpsed places such as this on those weekend drives that have so many other and dreadful things to offer. Yes, out of fields just such a church will assert itself. And there *are* times when you do come to a bridge across a river and it's usable. Not every bridge is made up – or *not* made up – of collapsed girders. And the mill . . . well, he can pretend it's that wide-eaved, half-timbered Bredeney one, its great wheel in use again. The miller has returned, and inside, the flour comes flying down a chute after the stones have pulverised the corn.

*Er mahlet das Korn zu dem täglichen Brot,*
*und haben wir dieses, so hat's keine Not.*

But here in Germany there *is* want. Everyone has said so: everyone continues to say so. Daily bread does not appear easily.

The boy plays with the village almost every day. He enjoys

the problems it poses – how big should the square be? should the church stand in it? where should the river that must flow under the bridge run? But often he is nagged at by a sense of verisimilitude. Most places *aren't* like the villages he makes. They aren't like it, because . . .

Very regretfully he must do it. He is someone who likes to be accurate. Indeed exactitude has beauty for him. Trembling a little at the sadness of it all, but also obeying this duty to truth, he pushes on to their sides certain arbitrarily chosen toy houses. Not enough! For – as his dream has made only too clear – how often do you come across a church that is standing in its entirety? So he lays flat the (detachable) church tower.

'Why,' asks his mother, 'have you knocked over pieces of your village?'

'I haven't knocked them over,' says the boy. 'It's just that there *must* be broken buildings. Otherwise it won't be like a real place.'

He sees he has given his mother pain, but he thinks: surely what I've said is true? Every normal place *does* have broken buildings, and a great many have very few that are not.

On any drive they are there, dreadfully to fill the hours and miles.


The chauffeur, Stumpfer, has shown him on the map where Essen is, at the centre-left of the Ruhr district. (Once the greatest industrial area in all Europe, says his father, and its steelworks and mines will make it so again.) To the west of Essen lie Mülheim, Oberhausen, Duisburg; to the east,

Bochum, Remscheid, Dortmund; to the north, Gelsenkirchen; and then to the south, Wuppertal, Solingen, Düsseldorf – with Köln, also called Cologne, further to the south. It's all Westfalen. They travel up and down it. But Mülheim (where the older English children go to school) turns out to be like Gelsenkirchen, which is the same as Oberhausen; Duisburg is no different from Dortmund, and all – against any hopes that, ever more dimly, the boy tries to entertain – are like the greater part of Essen itself. Like what it so bafflingly proffered that morning of arrival. *Broken buildings* making up a whole world and enclosing you, keeping away any other. Everything says No! and Nothing! and Not here! Not in the cities of Germany!

Stillness where bustle should be; heaps of stones where walls should rise; inaccessible spaces where rooms should welcome; gashed façades resembling broken teeth with the blackness of rot behind them instead of busy apartment blocks or tempting shops – and above them, giant and imperfect church towers that repeat the upright protrusions of metal beams in the debris. Rubble for floors, weeds for carpets, the exposed sagging of precarious storeys for balconies, the sky for roofs. And pervading the sprawling wretchedness a smell both sweet and acid, delivering desolation so pungently that the boy knows he'll never forget it, in all the years ahead of him. He does not yet know of what the smell is compounded.

Most weekends Stumpfer drives them to some place or other following signposts (both newly put-up ones, and those from the past with those curious thick old Gothic letters) down one street of unrelieved ruins to come out into yet another. A Somewhere is promised – Wuppertal, perhaps, or that city his parents knew before he was born and had admired so much, Köln – yet you always ended up in a Nowhere.

'You know why it's difficult to persuade people to move out of the central parts of the towns?' remarks his father to his mother (though they've seen scarcely anyone all trip, except for British soldiers directing traffic). 'It's because many of them think their men'll return from the East, from Russia, to where they were last living. The women stay on here in hope.'

So presumably in so far as Toni and Trude have homes, it's somewhere in this smashed-up immensity – to which their men might come back. Might! The boy knew that whatever they said, the two German women had not, in fact, given up hope. And what would the men themselves feel when, or if, they *did* return? To arrive in a broken street which they'd last seen when everything was whole, when there was noise, when there was movement, when there was life.


He has learned two new songs now. One is English, with an almost menacing tune (so many repeated notes!):

> Hark, Hark,
> The dogs do bark,
> The beggars are coming to town;
> Some in rags,
> Some in tags,
> And some in a velvet gown.

27

When he sings this song, he sees in his mind the little towns that Dr Ahlens's village resembles, those well to the south of the Ruhr cities and with little to no damage. They stand like islands of serenity and oldness in green, cultivated land. It's pleasant there. Yet often he can imagine armies of all the hungry, angry, homeless folk from Essen and her sisters storming them. And what would happen then? What would a St Martin do in those circumstances? Half a cloak wouldn't be much use . . .

The other song is German, with a slow, swelling melody: 'O Tannenbaum'. To address a tree in song makes you think it can hear you. Should it wish to, it could sing back to you, sing back some profound assurance that all is really well, whatever has happened in the world of men. He has been taught this second song because Christmas is coming and the *Tannenbaum* will be brought into the house, and an angel placed on its top. And when Christmas is over, it will return to Nature.

> *Du grünst nicht nur zur Sommerszeit,*
> *nein, auch im Winter, wenn es schneit.*
> *O Tannenbaum, o Tannenbaum,*
> *wie grün sind deine Blätter!*

(You are green not only in the summertime, no, also in winter, when it's snowing. O fir-tree, O fir-tree, how green are your leaves!)

In the sitting-room a *Krippe* (crib) is placed. It shows Jesus, the light of the world, newly born in a country stable, with oxen and donkeys kneeling by his cradle in homage. He was

God's son, but He also had human parents, caught here in painted wood, Josef and Maria, *die Jungfrau-Mutter*. Perhaps such a stable could be found in the more peaceful countryside beyond Cologne.

The boy notices that his mother doesn't really welcome questions about what the *Krippe* is all about.

Toni and Trude are both Roman Catholics, like almost everybody in Westfalen. His father says that, despite his own upbringing, he thinks the Roman Catholic Church the best, perhaps the only, institution for bringing the peoples of a shattered Europe together before the one God. He may even become a Catholic himself, and anyway will accompany Toni and Trude to Mass. 'What *would* your father have thought?' says the boy's mother to him. She herself goes to no church at all.


Dreadfully broken though it is, Düsseldorf is a place of far greater activity than any of the Ruhr cities. You can see lights and liveliness in its Königsallee. And there is a theatre to which the boy is taken to see a play: a pantomime called *Aladdin*.

He has not expected that the curtains will part to reveal a brightly lit and above all a *whole* world, thronged with merry-seeming people, sometimes talking, sometimes singing, and all wearing exotic clothes of gaudy colours. And the townscape behind them is so appealing: low houses painted in pinks and reds and tile-roofed, and in the distance a many-storeyed tower called a 'pagoda', because Aladdin lives in China. The boy remembers the name, 'China', and feels that it must be the most wonderful country there is. In the corner of the stage stands a tree; every time someone waters it, it shoots up. And Aladdin himself has a lamp which, when he rubs it, produces a genie who can grant his wishes.

If *he* had a wish it would be for all the cities and towns here to be mended again, to be as cheerful as Peking.

When he gets home, he tells Toni and Trude about the pantomime. They smile at him, and look at each other, in rather a knowing sort of way, and then say: 'Ach, Paul, how you'd enjoy a German *Kasperltheater*.'

He hears that in the New Year Stumpfer will be leaving them – they'll be having a new chauffeur, a young man called Matthias. Stumpfer will move back to Hamburg, where his family live.


Real towns were empty. In the town on the stage there'd been much cheerful coming and going, and so must there be in his toy village. So had there been in Broadway, Worcestershire: his mother misses her friends there. Of course in Tirpitzstraße itself, as well as in certain other Bredeney streets, there are English families, most of whom have young children. But his mother wants to see only a very few of them. Within the British community many parties are held, but she never wants to go to them, not to cocktail parties nor to 'do's at the Tennis Club. Nor the bridge mornings, nor receptions, often at the Villa Hügel itself, given by brigadiers and colonels for distinguished visitors from 'UK'. ('It's stupid this habit here of calling it "UK",' his mother says. 'It's England or Scotland or Wales or Ireland. Why have British people abroad got to develop such an affected way of talking!') His father says that, while he himself prefers the company of Germans, the real people of this country, he thinks that his wife should attend some of these British functions, and that they should have people round to dinner, especially during the Christmas/New Year season. His mother doesn't care for this idea at all. 'Oh well,' says his father, 'you haven't much to offer any company because you've so little grasp of what is going on.' And if the guests are German, then her command of the language is weak; her German is *falsch*, kitchen-German with, at best, a strong regional accent and idiom. Like Toni and Trude she invariably pronounces *ch* as *sch*; there are hardly any gutturals.

In fact his mother sees far more of Toni and Trude than of anybody else, and seems fairly content for things to be that way. *They* certainly don't mind whether her German is *falsch* or not, in fact Toni tells her that there is something very attractive about the way she speaks the language. But of course really she wants to be back in the English countryside – preferably the Cotswolds, but also Dorset, where she has a summer chalet, and Yorkshire where she grew up and where her family comes from. The only thing here she doesn't mind doing is riding – sometimes along the tracks in the great *Stadtwald* (municipal wood), which Essen, like so many big German cities, can boast, sometimes in the patches of countryside between the Ruhr towns.

Among all the English children, the boy knows best Hilary, the dark, vivacious little girl who lives in the adjoining house; the two Scottish boys, sons of his mother's one real friend here, Margaret Fleming; and Philip and Elspeth, with whom he will share lessons in the New Year. They're both his age. They tell him that, in the opinion of their parents, he spends far too much time with German servants.

Toni and Trude have quite a number of callers whom they receive in the kitchen, often members of the Deutsche Polizei, whose headquarters is in Tirpitzstraße, in one of its few buildings not inhabited by English people. They all love to sing together and often his mother stands outside the kitchen door to listen to their voices, so full-throated, so sensitively harmonious with each other. Sometimes the songs are rather jolly ones, with thumping rhythms:

> *Jeden Sonntagabend die Dorfmusik spielt,*
> *Und die Katherine geht immer!*

But more often than not the songs are laden with a sadness you can't exactly name. Each of the voices seems sad in its own way, yet sympathetic to the sadness of others:

> *Weißt du, wieviel Sternlein stehen*
> *an dem blauen Himmelszelt?*
> *Weißt du, wieviel Wolken gehen*
> *weithin über alle Welt?*

(Do you know how many stars there are in the blue canopy of heaven? Do you know how many clouds drift over all the world?)

The freezing night shows now a multitude of cold stars whose existence worries the boy because it surpasses his powers of understanding. But the song also reminds him of all the poor and hopeless people everywhere – those children, for example, who'd brought him Debs, multiplied by a hundred, a thousand, a million.

With Christmas at hand the songs that float from the kitchen quarters – from male and female, from young and old – increasingly commemorate the first one; they seem almost to breathe life into the wooden *Krippe*. Best of all, but also sad somehow – sad with a sense of distance and of difficulty and with the ambivalence of quiet – is:

> *Stille Nacht, heilige Nacht!*
> *Alles schläft, einsam wacht*
> *nur das traute hochheilige Paar.*
> *Holder Knabe im lockigen Haar,*
> *schlaf in himmlischer Ruh,*
> *schlaf in himmlischer Ruh!*

(Silent night, holy night! All is sleeping, only the beloved and most holy couple are awake. Pure-natured boy with curly hair, sleep in heavenly peace, sleep in heavenly peace!)

Though the carol is German, the boy's parents know English words to it; so here's a song – for once – that he can sing in *both* languages. You could, you might think, find a parallel between the Holy Family – father, mother, one son – and his own. But it wouldn't work. His parents are no *traute hochheilige Paar*: they quarrel more and more, and it's almost worse when they don't, so charged is the silence between them at mealtimes.

\*

33

On Christmas morning he finds the present he asked for, a football, but downstairs, in the dining-room, between the grandfather clock and the *Tannenbaum*, another one awaits him, from Toni and Trude. It fills him with a joy for which he cannot find the words: no better present will ever be given him. It's a *Kasperltheater* – a traditional Westphalian one – for himself. Its front has been redecorated – with coloured paper, patterned with sun, moon and stars. There are red curtains to part, just as in that pantomime-theatre in Düsseldorf. They disclose a bare stage – at the back of which he finds the entire cast of a *Kasperlspiel*.

They are glove puppets with brightly painted papier mâché heads: Kasperle himself, the German Punch, with an enormous nose, a red face and a stocking-cap; Gretchen, his gentle-faced, flaxen-haired, rosy-cheeked wife; the king, silver-bearded, with crimson robes and a splendid golden crown; the queen, whose sharp features are not dissimilar to Trude's, perhaps on one of her happier days, when she's decided that after all her man *could* come back from Russia alive; and a boy that could be himself, if he'd lived long ago here in Germany. There is a beneficence emanating from all these puppets, even from old Kasperle, though he looks so hot-tempered and really rather stupid. This is not the case, however, with the remaining two members of the cast. It is hard to say which of the two is the more alarming. Is it the *Hexe*, the witch – such as he has already met in Trude's book of fairy-tales, her face twisted in malevolence, her nose wrenched to one side, with one (open) eye higher than the other (closed) one, and two bad teeth protruding from her discoloured lips? Or is it the ghost, the *Gespenst* – bald, blind,

34

his head entirely white, except for the black blotches that are his eyes, nose and mouth? His cloak is black too. He is death-in-life.

The king is God, obviously. The witch and the ghost, however, also represent forces you can feel – like bitter winds blowing through the urban deserts of the Ruhr, moaning through the arches of the fallen houses, or else, in the countryside, making the fir-trees sigh in the dark woods, where so little grows on the sandy floor . . .

The cold increases. Then comes snow, and when, after days of fierce flurries, it's settled, everything freezes hard. Bredeney becomes beautiful, most trees cargoed with white and the sombre green firs all dressed in it. All the woodland walks have a strange pure softness about them now: your footsteps don't ring out, everything's muffled. The Villa Hügel, pinnacled in snow, looms up from its park more tremendously than ever. At the foot of its now unnegotiable terraces the Balderneysee is iced over; the young start trying their luck at skating on it.

There's a toboggan he can use, and near the lake, or close to the *Stadtwald*, are slopes for him to fly down – for it feels like flying, defying the flaky, biting wind that your own coursing downhill arouses. He becomes quite intrepid, always pointing his sledge down the sheerest incline he can find. Günter comes out with him. They enjoy it if the toboggan skids and careers and they perhaps even have to fall off it, tumbling into that whiteness that turns out not to be so soft after all, and makes your face smart. Being so much

35

older, Günter is a far better tobogganer than himself, and an even braver one, and the boy likes watching him manipulate the vehicle against chosen dangers, and emerge, usually unscathed, at the foot of the ride, his cheeks even redder than usual, his fair hair powdered with snow-dust.

It would be wonderful if the world could always be transfigured in this way. But his parents say no, it wouldn't be – he must understand that this winter, which threatens to be the severest of their lifetimes, will bring great suffering to many. Back in England people are hungry and cold, even when they're indoors; blizzards in the Channel are making ship-deliveries of goods both ways almost impossible. And if it's bad for the British, both in their own country and in Germany, think how much worse it already is, and is going to be, for the Germans here. We've got our work cut out getting them enough to eat as it is.

What is it that makes the position of the Germans so different from his own, and that of his parents and their Tirpitzstraße neighbours?


Certainly day after day of relentless icy wind lowers the spirits. His mother is a great believer in walks, and then Debs has to be exercised (the snow excited him at first, making him scamper about, but by now even he too has an almost resigned attitude to it), but their walks get shorter, more circumspect, of necessity. His mother joins an organisation that takes her into central Essen. Sometimes she is joined by women in strange bonnets and heavy dark coats. They are members of the Salvation Army, though they don't look much like members of that ordinary army, those the boy sees in the Villa Hügel. 'What people in *this* army believe, and what they publish in their magazine, that's nonsense,' says his mother. 'But what they do and are, that's another matter. They must be some of the most selfless people in the world – and certainly the most selfless in Germany now. They don't mind where they go, what diseases they expose themselves to . . . I shall remember it always.'

When his mother returns from these visits, she will take herself to her room – or go alone into the *Wintergarten* – and cry a little.


Matthias has arrived, and he is as different as can be from Stumpfer, young, lithe and very strong. He suggests some animal from books about the jungle, one who can outrun any quarry but who is also able to lie in wait, to gather together all the nerves in his well-disciplined, taut body and pounce. He likes driving the car as fast as he can, and his manner towards the boy's father is a familiar, pally one; often he'll put an arm round him or slap him on the back. To his surprise the boy sees that his father, normally so reserved, is pleased by such behaviour.

Matthias would like to play football with Günter and himself, and he'll help with a snowman in the garden or with putting new runners on the sledge.

But Matthias's face! Nobody prepared the boy for it, and he cannot decide whether he wants to turn his gaze from it or to study it hard. How can the eyes have stayed in place, when something must have torn skin and flesh and muscles away to leave only this multi-coloured mess – white, purple, red, like chunks of meat pressed uneasily together, and clinging awkwardly to a framework of bone? Matthias doesn't seem to mind about it, but what must he think when he looks at himself in the mirror? Was he *always* like that?

No, of course not! The reply is emphatic. Matthias is lucky to be alive. He was a Luftwaffe pilot and was shot down. He was badly burned; the doctors gave up hope. But he was astonishingly brave. He had his wife and his little son, Klaus, to think of; he was determined to live, you see.

Imagine being in an aeroplane when it catches fire! Think of the pain the flames must have caused him . . . The boy *does* imagine these things, casting his eyes up to the sullen-coloured winter sky when he hears the sound of a plane, and picturing this turning into a red ball, rolling through miles of cold air until it bursts upon the ground. Had been *shot down*. But who would want to shoot an aeroplane down?

Is it the awe he fills him with, on account of his ravaged face and strange experiences and untold bravery, or is it something else about Matthias that makes the boy feel uneasy with him? When Matthias is at last free to join him and Günter with their football, he plays with them in an almost menacing way, determined to do others down, to show himself off as wily and altogether superior. His driving's like that too – always overtaking, always swinging round corners. He often adjusts with his hands, with a shake of the body, the chauffeur's uniform he wears; you can tell he's proud of the way he carries it, with his broad shoulders and slim hips. Yet he's also often disconcertingly gentle and courteous, deferential to the boy's mother in a way she perhaps doesn't altogether like, and he plays with Debs as fondly as could be wished.

He always whistles before he comes into the kitchen – which he usually does on arrival at the house. (Every morning he collects the boy's father for work.) Toni and Trude pretend to think Matthias rather silly and boyish, but it's clear that they secretly like him. From time to time he joins in their singing. Strangely, it isn't the jollier songs he's good at but the tender ones: '*Weißt du, wieviel Sternlein stehen?*' for example.

The boy sees more of Philip and Elspeth now – for lessons, done mostly in the dining-room of Tirpitzstraße 49, with the heating as full on as it can be this winter, and the snow brightly reflected in the *Wintergarten* glass. And also for some walks through the woods and for games – weather permitting – in the garden. He doesn't like either of them very much: Philip says he wants to be a soldier, Elspeth keeps telling him how much she prefers Philip to himself. They both say he has a funny way of talking, often putting German words into sentences or giving English words (like the past participles of verbs) German forms. It all comes from mixing too much with the servants.

'In our house,' says Elspeth, 'we're always careful to lock things away from the Germans who work for us. My mother looks every day to see whether something has gone from any of the cupboards because, even in the few minutes they're open, those Germans might have helped themselves.

They're often asking for things to eat! Why *should* they have more than they've got already?'

There comes the afternoon – inevitably – when the boy raises the subject of the broken buildings of Essen. What made them like that? Who did the breaking?

'Why, *we* did, of course!' Elspeth and Philip say in chorus.

' "We"?'

'We British! We destroyed all those places!' ('Destroyed': perhaps the ugliest word there is. And the wickedest.)

'Why would we want to do that?'

'Because the Germans were our enemies! They *are* our enemies . . .'

He has to ask his parents what 'enemy' means: it's a word that belongs to the past, they say, but he knows it doesn't. What Philip and Elspeth have told him was a fact.


To live with this knowledge – how will it be possible? Has it come as a total surprise, or had, somewhere in deep regions of his being, all those looks and unfinished sentences and incomprehensible words united to hint at the appalling truth? How can he ever go again into the centre of Essen without an unbearable sense of shame softening his loins, drying his mouth, filming his eyes over? How will he ever be able to stand another car journey, knowing that the forlorn town-scapes he's passing through were brought about by his own people?

A car trip such as he's never made before follows very soon after.

The boy is to meet his parents in the grand hall of the Villa

Hügel, and Matthias will drive him there. He follows the young man into the car. Matthias explains that he won't drive to the Villa straight away – they have plenty of time – but will go first into the middle of Essen. He has to pick up something from his home.

The boy tries to steel himself against entry into the terrible maze he knows to lie ahead, the more terrible for the snow that has now heaped itself upon it. Snow beautifies woods, suburbs, old cities, graces trees and towers and statues, but it makes the desolation of destroyed Essen only the greater. Grubby and hard, it's piled behind the scorched façades whose black stains it emphasises, is visible through the hollows that simulate windows to mock at dreams and memories of a warm, well-lit life behind walls and glass, secure from winter's cold.

Inside the maze Matthias stops the car. Here we are, Paul. *Here!* The boy looks at him incredulously. How could anyone really be *living* here? Matthias points up a gap between frozen heaps of debris to where a light shines through the dull twilight – from a tiny fragment of a house overshadowed by ghastly arches of once bigger buildings. 'Yes, this is my house! Please, come and see it. I'd like you to meet my wife, and my little son, Klaus.'

So: Matthias and his family are living like animals in an impoverished burrow amid ruins that we British have made.

It is unthinkable to get up out of the car and go into this place. His shame is too great. He shakes his head; he'd rather stay here, thank you. 'But my wife and small boy would so like to meet you,' says Matthias. 'I've told them such a lot about you.'

He feels a tearing at his heart. But he simply cannot go into that house of Matthias's for all the imploring look on his face. A second time he shakes his head. Matthias tries to smile, the white blotches on his face glow with emotion. The boy knows he is hurt, very hurt. This pains him – he shivers – actually it *is* cold, even inside the car – and he lowers his head so that he can't meet Matthias's eyes.

Left to himself, he wishes himself away – to Aladdin's Peking, to his toy village, jolly and intact amid serene countryside, even back to England, where ruins are surely quite unknown. But it's impossible to vanquish these present mournful surroundings; he is their prisoner. Perhaps he always will be.

And now there comes a tap at the window. Matthias is back, and by his side is a young woman, his wife (there can be no doubt of that from the way they stand together). She it is who has tapped, and she does so again. The boy winds the window down, and she brings her face through the blast of cold towards his. If he really doesn't want to come inside, she says, won't he accept this? 'Yes, *please, mein liebe Paul,*' says Matthias. She brings forth from the folds of her apron an apple, and smiles at him, as if to assure him of something (though what?). Her own face is itself rather like an apple: polished, round, red-cheeked, ripe, sweet. He takes the fruit from her, and smiles his strongest at her and at Matthias, kindly with the icy, gathering dust behind them.

A sorrow fills him that he knows will not ever quite pass away, and which no screams or tears can express. He has entered the realm where the *Gespenst* is sovereign.

**42**

# Two

He has, he knows, to be more persistent in his questioning: he has made it far too easy for people to fob him off. Just as, not so long ago, he came into possession of this country's language, so must he come into possession of what happened in it while he himself was still living in Broadway, Worcestershire. It *was* the British who broke the cities, wasn't it? Philip and Elspeth were *not* making things up. All right, the British-and-the-Americans (he has seen American visitors at the Villa Hügel), but it *was* the British, none the less. Why did they (why did *we*) do it? *How* did they (how did *we*) do it? Paul, there are some things . . . Up in the rose-patterned isolation of his bedroom he works hard at putting together the ill-shaped pieces of a verbal jigsaw (for he asks anyone he can).

At one time (though when?) the British were in Britain, the Germans in Germany. Members of one country went to another for holidays (such as he's been taken on inside Germany, to the Harz mountains, to the Siebengebirge) or for work (such as the occasional visits his father makes to Hamburg and Berlin). Then came the war, and now the word's ceased being a name for the period of living in Broadway and having a Mickey Mouse gas mask; instead it suggests other quite terrifying pictures. The British and the Germans take off for each other's country, are flying at each other in unleashed fury (he thinks repentantly of temper tantrums of his own); the boy sees the two peoples as flocks of birds, of fiery birds – no, of aeroplanes, aiming to collide with one another or to cause their opposite number to fall down in flames. (In one of those planes brave Matthias sits, his face young and still handsome; then the British topple him from the skies, and he lands, with much of his skin off, and big chunks of flesh too.) And he isn't very far wrong either. Mostly, his father explains reluctantly, batting his eyelids in annoyance at all these questions, the cities were broken, as you call it, from the air. Later some were burned from the ground. And some things like the bridges were destroyed – blown up – by British soldiers, as they marched into Germany.

But wasn't all that very wicked? Yes, extremely wicked, says his father. In the east of Germany there was perhaps the most beautiful city in all Europe: Dresden. In a night and a day British and American aeroplanes flattened it completely: 130,000 people died, and the whole world lost one of its treasures.

And *he* is British – and speaks the same language as the Americans! He wants to hide himself from Toni, Trude, Hannelore, Günter, out of sorrow for what his countrymen have done.

But who among them did it? Not his father, who'd been in Broadway and had nothing to do with military matters.

His father had mentioned soldiers, though – who'd blown up bridges across the Rhine, who'd maybe set fire to towns and villages he'd seen. And most days he meets men who are in the Army: brigadiers, colonels, lieutenant-colonels. Among them there has to be – it only stands to reason – one who participated in the devastation – yes, even of Essen itself.

They are not to escape: *he* will bomb too, with honest questions that require honest answers. He now knows that 'bombing' is the best word to use: 'broken buildings' is too childish.

'Hello, Paul!'

'Hello. I want to ask you something.'

'Anything you care to, old chap!'

'Did *you* have anything to do with the bombing?'

'What was that?'

'Did *you* have anything to do with the damage to Essen?'

'Well, actually, no, old man.'

'Do you know anyone who did?'

'I'm sorry?'

'Do *you* know people who *did* bomb Essen?'

'We'ell . . .'

'You must do; you're in the Army, aren't you?'

'Well yes, but . . .'

'Doesn't the Army burn things and blow them up?'

'Well, I wouldn't put it *quite* like that.'

'But in the Army there are people who fought the Germans?'

'I say,' (to the boy's mother), 'he does go on a bit, doesn't he?'

Here's Geoffrey from next door, father of nice, dark-haired Hilary.

'Hello, Paul. How are you?'

'Were you in the Army in the war? *My* Daddy wasn't.'

'As a matter of fact I was.'

'In Germany?'

'No.'

'Do you know people who *were* in Germany?'

'Sure, yes.'

'Do you know any now?'

'Well, of course.'

'Do you know men who bombed or burned places?'

'I don't think that . . . ?' (impatient).

'Do you know men who dropped *bombs*?'

'Bombs on where, old man?'

'On Essen.'

'On Essen? No!'

'But on other places?'

'What other places?'

'Dortmund, Mülheim, Gelsenkirchen. Places near Essen.'

'No!'

'On Hamburg?' the boy knows the names of all the major cities.

'Perhaps I may . . .'

'Dropping bombs on Hamburg's the same thing as dropping bombs on Essen, isn't it? Breaking the Germans' houses.'

'Here, you're going a bit, aren't you?'

'I want to *know* about things.'

'There are some, things, old man, it's best *not* to know

**46**

about at your stage in life. You ought to be enjoying yourself with – with your sledge and your football.'

'I want to know *why* British people dropped bombs. On where Toni and Trude come from?'

'Old man, I said wait till you're older!'


He is told that he has made Matthias very sad and that if – *if* – he were to be invited to his home again, he must accept.

And, of course, Matthias does ask him, and he has no choice but to follow him into the car . . . The winter will surely now last for ever. If anything, the snow in the derelict city centre is deeper, wider and thicker-crusted than on his first visit, the sky over it more leaden, the decay in the splintered-teeth buildings more advanced. How slippery the passage leading to Matthias's home is, with its film of ice! And how the wind slashes at your face! Matthias opens a door in what seems a wall's precarious survival; the boy's heart thumps.

But inside, the two tiny rooms with the damp-blotched walls are bright, snug – pleasant enough shelter from sadness and unkind weather. Everything shines, from the stove which heats them to the plates set out upon the table, from the framed photos of a Matthias with his face still complete to the pieces of linoleum laid on the floor.

Matthias's wife and his son, Klaus, seem strangely pleased at their English boy-visitor. But Matthias is the most pleased of all: his happy smile stretches broadly into the slabs of discoloured meat that form so much of his face. And then a horrible thought occurs to the boy. Matthias was in the

47

Luftwaffe. That's why he is as he is. Therefore he too must have been up there in the sky with the sole purpose of dropping bombs on houses, homes, churches, railways – bombs that brought death to buildings and people alike. And now he is living in just such a ruin as perhaps he helped to make.

His head reels. He can bear no further thoughts. *Liebe Paul, liebe Paul* . . . But he wants to leave not only the tiny home and its grinning head, but Essen, Bredeney, everywhere. Perhaps back to the England he doesn't really remember . . . Perhaps just himself and Debs in a great wood, softened by snow: in his favourite story from Trude's book *Hänsel and Gretel*, he has always felt a certain envy of the brother and sister, cast adrift from humankind in the populated solitude of the woods.


He doesn't like eating: really he'd rather not eat at all. Yes, obviously he likes a ring-shaped, sugar-dusted *Kuchen* from Toni and the *Klöse* (dumplings) she puts in stews, and fruit when it comes his way, but otherwise . . . Meat is horrible, because it means animals have died. And who could like tinned vegetables? Drinking is little better than eating. There's only disgusting condensed milk (German cows might be carrying tuberculosis). And water has to be boiled before you can drink it; think of the chaos the German sewage system is in, after all the bombing!

And anyway mealtimes are the occasions when his parents look frostily across the dining-room table at one another, or deliberately don't meet each other's eyes . . .

It's disgraceful that the boy won't eat! Literally *millions* of Germans are near starvation this dreadful winter, not to mention Russians, Poles, all the displaced people in the encampments. Even Toni, perhaps offended by his reaction to her careful cooking, joins in the chorus of reprimands. *Paul ist unzufrieden.* (Paul is discontented.)

But at last the cold lets up, the snows melt, spring comes. Snowdrops appear, shy, delicate yet defiant, down below the grotto in the gardens of the Villa Hügel, as well as in the woods. Day by day these woods transform themselves, become full of sounds and activities, their gradual green self-covering renders them more mysterious as well as more inviting, a more complete alternative, a more effective challenge to that other world, the ruined one, the city-world, the world in which British and Germans flew at each other. They take walks, his mother, Debs and himself, more often now in the spacious *Stadtwald* with its plenitude of paths.

Of all the flowers he's shown, as spring moves forward into the year, one kind above all others makes an impression on him, with its cup-like shape and its fragrance, almost more like a melody than a smell: the *Maiglöckchen*. *Glöckchen*, little bells; *Mai*, the month of May (and a final end to the punishments imposed by winter, singing out sweetly all over the German woods). He keeps on forgetting the flower's much less interesting English name: 'lily of the valley'.

When the rain comes down, whether in downpours or in showers (as in April and May), it's fun to sing with Hannelore, '*Es regnet, es regnet, die Erde wird Naß*' 'It's raining, it's raining, the Earth will be wet) with its pleading, perhaps impertinent chorus:

> *Mach mich nicht naß,*
> *mach mich nicht naß,*
> *mach nur die bösen Kinder naß.*

(Don't make me wet, don't make me wet, make only the bad children wet.)

(But then *he* is bad too, as he's never been before, refusing to eat, not desisting from asking embarrassing questions . . .) And when the sun breaks through the woods and bird-song fills them, and he can hear, for the first time since he learned that favourite song of his, the twofold call of the cuckoo, then they'll sing together:

> *Kuckuck, Kuckuck, ruft's aus dem Wald.*
> *Lasset uns singen,*
> *tanzen und springen!*
> *Frühling, Frühling wird es nun bald.*

(Cuckoo, cuckoo! is heard from through the wood. Let us sing, dance and jump about! Spring, spring will soon be here.)

In the towns the weeds flower and put forth green tentacles that spread across the rubble and all over the fallen masonry and shattered walls. Even a desert shows a change in season. When the skies are blue, with fleecy white clouds blown across them, the bombers of the Ruhr are rebuked afresh for what they did, for the insult to Nature they so relentlessly delivered.

50

'Hello, Paul!'

'I'd like to ask you a question.'

'Not the same one again, I hope, old man.'

'How many British people, and how many Americans, are living in Germany now?'

'I really couldn't tell you.'

'Someone must know!'

'I'm sure someone does, but *I* don't.'

'But there are quite a lot!'

'You could say that, yes, old chap.'

'So among them there must be *one* person who did damage to all the buildings?'

'Probably, probably.' To the boy's mother: 'I really think you should take him to a trick cyclist.'

Boy's mother: 'Well we *have* thought about doing so, I must admit. But then you can look at it another way: Paul's right, isn't he? People *are* around who took part in the bombing. Of course the boy's got a bit strange with his persistent questions and bad dreams . . .'

When the guest had gone: 'Mummy, you agree with me then? And the British were very wicked, weren't they?'

'Oh, Paul,' (a little exasperatedly), 'what about Coventry? What about London, Portsmouth, Hull, Bristol, Exeter, Plymouth? Think about that. Hull, where *my* family came from; Bristol, where Daddy's family once lived. Bombed too, even if not quite in the way the places here were.'

But England stays in his mind as that amiable village – with an oak-beamed tea-shop at the end of your afternoon walk.

Quite often now they go to stay in Bad Godesburg, in a

hotel called the Petersburg, itself high up amid woods and handsome villas, with views of the hills called the Siebengebirge, which were once giants, and of the huge Rhine flowing past, carrying heavily loaded barges towards Cologne, towards Holland and the open sea and England. His father seems markedly more cheerful and friendly in these surroundings and tells him about the Rhine's journey and what lies – temptingly discernible – just to the south of where they are, a country of sheer cliffs and castles perched on them and vineyards and small red-roofed villages at their feet with quays to receive the boats and their passengers. The whole area is full of history, he says, and the boy senses that here history means something other than the war and what made Germans and British attack one another. Its very remoteness makes it almost beautiful. And history can produce ruins – like those of the Drachenfels, so mysterious at sunset – which do not chill and depress like those of Essen.

One Saturday he is told that the drive Matthias is taking them on will be a longer one than usual. They're going to see some people who live near Aachen, a city close to the Belgian border, but who are connected with friends back in Broadway. This visit is a *very* important one so he must promise to be good. And he must eat anything he's given. The boy nods miserably.

Aachen is as shattered, as desolate as Essen – as Dortmund, Duisburg, Cologne. Then they leave it to re-enter more vital countryside, and come to the object of their journey – a castle.

Its copper-green turrets gleam in the sun; there is a moat, the waters of which have a green coverlet of lily-pads, and a drawbridge.They drive over this to find themselves in a quiet courtyard; between its paving-stones the grasses grow. Couldn't this be the castle of the Sleeping Beauty? – under a spell?

Here the stillness is different from that of the cities; somehow the boy knows that this strange, unexpected place not only *has* been loved but *is still loved*, for all its unkemptness. That makes things different.

If there's enchantment here, it's broken very quickly. Out of an old, studded door come people who greet them with apparently incredulous delight. What good, kind English people to be coming all this way to see Germans, and in these circumstances! And people who have *actually seen* . . . and names follow of relations, who went to live in England before the war, whom the boy's parents had befriended. Thanks be to God!

They follow their hosts into a large, flag-floored kitchen. There's an elderly man and two women, of the same age, one talkative, the other sad and silent though smiling. This kitchen too is like something in Trude's fairy-tale book, with its large dresser and its great black stove and the open fireplace up which you can look, through bird's nests, to a tiny piece of sky. Waffles are produced: here's something to eat the boy really *does* like! Talk then settles down, like birds on their clutches of eggs, upon one topic: the whereabouts and predicament of two people, a mother and a son, and what Daddy and Mummy can do to help them. What they've been through, how they've suffered, what an evil time these last years have truly been. The bombs were almost the best part of it . . . Glances are given in the boy's direction. There's so much it's best for the boy not to know. Yes, says his mother, we've judged that wisest. Anyway, to go on with the matter in hand . . . This mother is called Finette, the boy Joachim or Achim. As the talk becomes more specific, more detailed, the elderly man leads the boy out into the untidy garden that lies to the back of the *Schloss* but is still separated by the moat from the rest of the world. Chickens scrabble about, and there are hutches of rabbits, brown ones like the wild variety, not the fluffy white-patched domestic kind. He's invited to shove leaves through wire netting for animals he knows without being told are doomed – destined for the meagre table in the castle kitchen. As he does so, he thinks about this pair being so ardently discussed inside. What is it exactly they've been through? It's obviously something a little different from the experiences of Toni and Trude, and perhaps most other inhabitants of Essen. He plies the elderly man with questions, not aggressive ones like those to the Englishmen encountered in the Villa Hügel, but nevertheless not uninformed by anxiety: who *are* Finette and Achim, and what is there about them for his parents to discuss?

The elderly man says, 'When you meet them, Paul, you must be *very* kind to them.'

Finette and Achim – they stand out in the imaginable near-future like two castle towers in the Rhineland, charged with some indefinable and alluring quality.


He likes stories, poems, pictures that celebrate the secret yet purposeful, and all-but-hidden lives of the denizens of woods and fields – squirrels, badgers, rabbits, hares, hedgehogs, mice, voles, rats, owls, woodpeckers, frogs, toads. A hedgehog (invisible to everyone but him) becomes his constant companion, and he also often pretends to be a mouse/rat, making himself whiskers and ears out of Plasticine and a long tail out of his pyjama-cord.

In the story of Hänsel and Gretel he is very impressed by the way non-human creatures help the two abandoned children (though admittedly birds are guilty of eating up the peas that Hänsel strews as the two of them are led further into the forest). But a dog mourns for them; rabbits and, above all, deer befriend them, and it is a duck who carries first Hänsel, then Gretel, across the stream after they've escaped the witch. Fir forests he now always calls 'Hänsel-and-Gretel woods' and feels some not wholly benign – though compelling – spirit emanating from them. Therefore he prefers deciduous woods.

To harm – let alone kill – the wood's natural inhabitants – what a dreadful crime that is and how incredible that anyone should want to do it. Yet . . .

He goes to the house next door, to play with Hilary. Geoffrey, her father, has just returned from an expedition to the forest, and he has brought back to Bredeney a trophy, which he can see if he follows him down to the cellar. It is a most beautiful stag, its russet, muscular body – suggesting, at one and the same time, great gentleness and great strength – dappled with blood, and its eyes, also blood-flecked, shining even in their blind lifelessness with reproach.

And the boy realises that something very evil and wanton

has been done (even though Geoffrey himself is amicable enough) and that it's related to bombing raids on cities and the blowing-up and burning of bridges and farms . . .

He perceives that his parents – both of them – agree with his noisy, unambiguous protests. But they tell him he mustn't express his feelings so vehemently, that it's high time he learned to control himself.

In that book of strange verses and pictures, *Struwwelpeter*, there's none he likes better than that of the hare, having his revenge on the hunter by depriving him of spectacles and gun, and turning the weapon on him.


Finette and Achim, Finette and Achim: still the talk about this mother and son goes on. Though it stops when he enters the room. And it's always in English. Here *is* something that both his father and mother do not want the Germans in the household to hear.


Hannelore has taught him an action-song – to be performed on the terrace overlooking the burgeoning garden:

> *Brüderlein, komm, tanz mit mir!*
> *Beide Hände reich ich dir,*
> *Einmal hin, einmal her,*
> *rundherum, das ist nicht schwer.*
>
> *Mit den Händen klapp, klapp, klapp,*
> *mit den Füßen trapp, trapp, trapp!*

*Einmal hin, einmal her,*
*rundherum, das ist nicht schwer.*


(Little brother, come, dance with me! Both hands I extend to you, one time there, one time here, round and round, it isn't difficult. With the hands, clap, clap, clap, with the feet, stamp, stamp, stamp! One time there etc.)

He is not Hannelore's little brother, but by the end of the year, he *will* be a brother to someone. In December – which seems unimaginably far ahead – a sister will arrive, and her name will be Prudence Elizabeth.


And Finette and Achim have, after so much expectation and preparation, arrived. They are given the bedroom next to the boy's own; there's a connecting door. The boy senses that Toni and Trude – and perhaps even Matthias – are somehow displeased by these new arrivals. Why? They are, after all, German, and now German is spoken all the time and everywhere in the house: it seems to him that only with Philip and Elspeth does he use the other language. For some reason he minds this.

His father is very attentive to Finette, asks her questions, always answers her, jokes (as he's never been known to do before), looks at her long and smilingly, behaves, in other words, entirely differently from usual. The German that comes rolling from his mouth acquires in her presence a new, a rather exclusive quality, for the boy doesn't always follow what's being said nor does he quite understand the nature of this changed and persistent rhythm. Mealtimes are worse than ever; he doesn't eat a thing. When his father presses the bell by his foot for the next course, his plate is usually as full as when it was brought him.

His mother, and Toni too, look at him reproachfully, but Finette often feels called on to comment. How glad she and her Achim would have been, all these long harsh years, for just one *quarter* of that meal! How extremely ungrateful to Providence it is to spurn what you can have so easily.

Over in her own Berlin . . . hunger, famine. Hasn't the boy grasped the situation in Germany? He should be *made* to eat up. Here, Toni, don't take his plate away! It shouldn't be removed until all its contents have disappeared into his mouth . . . Toni glowers; his mother, rather unusually for her, looks dithery, even helpless. 'Perhaps just another mouthful,' she pleads.

'In a Displaced Persons' camp such luxury,' Finette indicates the unappetising, congealing food in front of him, 'would be almost unimaginable.'

'Yes, unimaginable!' chips in his father. 'Eat it up, Paul. I'm getting pretty tired of this performance.'

'He's a little tense,' says his mother. 'Back in Broadway he was very different. Always laughing and running about and playing with the football. Here . . . he's a bit upset by things.'

Finette throws back her head and peals with mirth. 'Yes, yes I can see that,' she says. 'Excuse me, but it's all so very amusing. Yes, it must be *most* upsetting for him to be living here,' and she waves her hand to indicate the comfortable dining-room, with the comfortable drawing-room on the one side and the comfortable *Wintergarten* on the other. 'Oh, yes, very upsetting indeed!'

'Muriel,' says his father – and his eyelids bat away more irritatedly than ever – 'how *can* you say such stupid things? To compare Paul's problems to those Finette and Achim have had to endure – them and hundreds of thousands, no, *millions* of others! It's outrageous. It's an insult, an all too typically *British* attitude. It almost calls for an apology.'

'There,' says Finette, extending a hand to his father, 'there, John, there's no need to get angry on *my* behalf. Or on Achim's. I know that Muriel did not mean to be offensive. It's so difficult, it seems, for people to realise how things have been for us.'

His mother – who has an alarming temper when the boy's been naughty, with eyes that can flash like flares – casts her eyes down, looks wretched. 'Excuse me if I say the wrong thing,' she is mumbling. She's glad of a change of subject, which is perhaps as well, because she gets one. Finette turns the talk to the days of her Potsdam youth, when all was real elegance, culture and sophisticated fun, a world very different from the boy's mother's own early life in Yorkshire and Dorset villages (where her widowed mother worked first as a hospital matron and, later, as a district nurse). Important people – writers, musicians, politicians – are mentioned, droppers-in to Finette's long-gone home, whom his father clearly knows all about and whom his mother, equally clearly, has never heard of.

Finette is beautiful – even the boy can see that – with her tumble of black hair, her large, sad, liquid, near-black eyes and her full mouth. But her skin is very sallow, there are hollows in her cheeks, and she is thin – extraordinarily thin. Often she breaks into fits of coughing that convulse her, contorting her whole body with their violence and pain. Sometimes, recovering from one of these, she looks gaspingly up with watering eyes and salivating mouth as if to say: Doesn't what I'm afflicted with now excuse me everything? Who would want to change their lot with mine?

All the same, the boy cannot like her. Has he not seen the way she glances at his mother, half gloating, half contemptuous? And once he found his mother sitting on the sofa in the drawing-room, the *Wintergarten* windows behind her, with a dismal, hopeless expression on her face. She pretended she had not been crying, but it was evident that she had. What was the matter? 'Finette,' she said. 'Finette wants to take your father away from you and me.'

But in a sense she has already done this: at weekends now Matthias frequently drives the boy's father, Finette and Achim into the countryside, leaving his mother and himself back in Bredeney.


There's one walk he likes better than any other, and he tests his mother's patience by asking to go on it very often, particularly on one of the days when his father is out with Finette. In the middle of one of the woods above the Balderneysee, there's a railed-off area, which, once upon a time, you could have entered through a turnstile. That turnstile is now quite fast, as choked with plants and briars as the plantation into which it formerly led. 'Plantation', because the trees stand wider apart than in the wood proper; otherwise all is unkempt. But here and there, at intervals whose regularity would be better perceived if you could see the whole place, there are great cages of rusty iron, some roofed, some not, all harbouring wild growths of leaves, instead of the animals they must once have contained. 'I think it must have been a menagerie,' his mother says. But sometimes it seems to the boy that it still is, or rather that it remembers – and therefore can project – its former identity. He can hear, he thinks, scratchings, low bayings, buttings against iron bars, impatient movements and requests; he can see paws protruding through the gaps, and feral eyes shining brightly among the deceptive bushes. Where *had* all the animals gone to, who'd once been pent up here? What had befallen all the captive creatures when the rain of fire fell down?

The most rapacious tiger, the greediest snake, the fiercest wildcat had done nothing – had thought nothing and known nothing – which could have earned them their terrible ends in uncomprehending agony. And the gentler animals . . . the deer, such as Geoffrey next-door slaughtered, seem to be running towards him from the thickets, abolishing cage-and zoo-railings with their delicate determination.

'One day,' the now wild menagerie whispers, 'one day . . .'


'It's a wonder Finette's alive still!' remarks his father, after she has been cruelly racked by coughing yet again.

'Yes, yes, it is!' says his mother, pained, despite herself, by the other woman's pain.

His father doesn't think the boy is friendly or polite enough to their guests. Several times, for example, he's attempted to talk English (English!) in front of them.

The boy realises that there's truth in his father's rebuke (though he feels something of a traitor to his mother as he does so). Guilt almost invariably expresses itself in the sensation he has between his legs, all his private parts jellifying, it seems. Perhaps he should make amends to Finette and Achim. He has, as his parents continually tell him, so much, Achim so very little – and before their arrival in Tirpitzstraße things were even bleaker for the mother and son. A gesture, a sacrifice, is clearly expected of the boy by God, the *Kasperltheater* king with his glinting gold crown and keen eyes and crimson robe that envelopes the whole world . . .

One afternoon – all day there's been a light rain to which the trees in the garden have offered up their cups of blossom, and a coldness in the air which makes indoors preferable to outside – he decides that he must not postpone his moment of kindness any longer. He remembers St Martin who parted with one half of his cloak, his most precious (and necessary) possession. He should do likewise. He walks round and round his bedroom picking up things he likes, things he cannot imagine his solitary hours without: his green railway engine, a much-played pack of cards (from Margery Abbott's progressive toy-shop in London; they all bear bold, curious, semi-abstract devices, his favourite being one he calls 'ducks-in-electricity') and – forcing himself to – even one or two houses from Dr Ahlens's village and two of his 'soft animals', the hare with the long, erect ears, the soft and cuddly rabbit. (He is, to be honest, rather glad that the puppet-theatre is downstairs.) All these objects he holds in his arms with some difficulty, and then he opens the connecting door, into the room now occupied by Finette and her son (the very room, in fact, from which all those months ago he watched the St Martin's Eve procession). He knows that both of them are in there.

Finette is sitting on her bed, in an attitude almost habitual to her when she is off guard; her back is bent, her head droops as in some immeasurable despair. Her downcast eyes seem to be finding some grim souvenir of her past at her feet. She turns round at the boy's entrance, startled, then surprised and not a little annoyed. (She guards this room – in *his* house – very jealously.)

'These are *all* for Achim,' he says, and there's a martyr's pride in his voice.

'How could they be?' she says. 'They're yours. They've been given to *you*.'

'But I want Achim to have them.' Words that both his mother and his father have used come into his head. 'He has so little, and I have so much . . .'

The light in Finette's large eyes is very far from kind. Indeed, for all her never-deniable prettiness, she resembles for a moment the *Hexe* from his toy theatre.

'Take them away, Paul. He doesn't – we don't want them.'

'But –'

'Take them away, and please leave us alone. We were wanting a little time to ourselves, my boy and I. We need it, living in somebody else's house . . .'

Between his legs he goes soft again. Before he's made it back to the connecting door – rather awkwardly, for the toys are trying to slip from his folded arms now – Finette has broken into another of her fits of violent coughing. Each cough is like a hammer striking at her chest and sending excruciating reverberations all over her skeleton-thin body. 'It's a wonder she's alive', he thinks to himself.

But even as he feels sorry for her in her pain, he also feels a stab of hatred. He's tried his best to be good to her, and to Achim as well, and he's been rewarded by no word of thanks, only by snubs and angry eyes. It is as if the beggar had handed back St Martin his cloak. He will tell his mother about her ingratitude. Which, in fact, will justify his behaviour at mealtimes.


One afternoon he's taken by friends of his parents to see the arrival in Mülheim of a Scottish regiment, the Black Watch. He knows that Scotland is a part of Britain, attached to England, and is told during the car ride there of the interesting customs it's preserved. They wait in the desolation of Mülheim, surrounded by caved-in buildings, for the advent of the Scottish soldiers, and inevitably his mind travels back to last November, to waiting with Toni and Trude for St Martin and his retinue. But how different *this* occasion is! It isn't a carol of a man's goodness that is borne on the wind and then swells into melody, jubilantly filling the street, but inhuman, weird wheezings and wailings, the bagpipes that are carried by stern, skirted men who – whatever they are *really* like – appear before the assembled fellow British as if to carry out the harshest wishes of them all. March and music both suggest a ruthless rejection of joy, gentleness, ease, fun, the spurtings-forth of Nature, and accordingly a chill seizes the boy. Straight away he links these military Highlanders with the ghastly broken city about him, and he wants, with a desperation hard to control, to leave, to forsake the small, admiring crowd. He'd like to yell out, but he doesn't. You don't do such things in public, only in sleep, to break the power of dreams.

At times his yells are like the bird in that good, sweet song '*Kommt ein Vogel geflogen*': each one carries a message, a *Brieflein im Schnabel* (a little letter in its beak) from himself, trapped in that version of the real world which is filling and tormenting his head, where towns are all flames and are about to devour him. Sometimes, nowadays, he is confronted by men stepping into or out of aeroplanes, either just about to commit their crimes or – worse still – with the flush of their recent accomplishment suffusing their faces. Some of these men are Americans: Americans have turned up at the Villa Hügel of late, his father has met with them in Frankfurt and in Berlin, and – more generally – they occur, not very favourably, in his parents' conversation, almost as much as the Russians indeed. But they appear in his dreams, principally because whenever the boy alludes to British bombing of German cities his father – with increasingly resentful emphasis – reminds him of the Americans' participation in this, until he grows to hold them even more responsible. (And more strangely so, since America is not in Europe.)

After one such dream he has shrieked himself awake to realise that the trouble is not yet over, that the trembles the dream scenes have given him are not going to pass. Down below him he can hear the voices of his parents and Finette, agitated German sentences not completely distinguishable but charged with some feeling very nearly as disagreeable as

65

that informing the city of his sleep. He puts on his scarlet dressing-gown and makes his own way down the stairs, through the hall and dining-room and so into the drawing-room.

There the three of them are, momentarily frozen in a grim tableau – his mother lying in a swoon, flat on the floor, and, standing above her on either side, Finette and his father, the beams of their eyes meeting in guilty alliance. Fixed in the intensity of their drama, the protagonists are unable so much as to notice the boy who is its involuntary witness.

He will never forget what he's seen, he determines. And indeed the scene in the drawing-room hangs before him throughout lunch the next day, which, though Toni has put the *Klöse* he likes into the stew, seems more unappetising – more actually inedible – than usual.

'He must be *made* to eat it up,' observes Finette, as the boy has anticipated. 'When I think of my Achim, and how . . .'

His next remark will take them all by surprise. 'I don't want to speak in German any more,' he says, continuing to use the language, however. 'Why should I? I am an English boy.'

Finette leans back in malicious merriment at it all. 'Excuse me! But how funny it all is! Has nobody then *told* the boy that he comes on his father's side from a *German* family? Why not, I wonder?' She leans gleefully forward across the table. 'Paul, you have a German surname and, from your grandfather, German ancestors. Your *mother* may be English,' she waves a hand as if to dismiss the importance of this, 'but your *father* . . . why, *he's* something of a German: he looks German, he sounds German, I could sense it all *at once*! And you *are* your father's son . . .'

**66**

# Three

Beyond the lawn – on the middle of which the magnolia-tree grows, and also the horse-chestnut with his swing attached to it – is the kitchen garden, a perfect grid of paths criss-crossing at right angles, with fruit-bushes or vegetable patches between them. Old Peter's always at work here: 'Far, far more than what we pay him demands,' says the boy's mother, 'but then he's always worked here. It's his life.' Always? Certainly the cross, white-stubbled old man suggests measureless old age. How strange, though, to think of all these plants, whose produce is so sweet and benevolent, flowering and bearing fruit while bombs are dropping and people dying in nearby houses. And to think too of Peter himself labouring away, keeping beds dug and weedless, trees pruned and bushes in shape.

Here, out of doors, eating is another matter. The fruit that offers itself delights him: the way it appears among the leaves, the sensation of having it in his hands, the miracle it constitutes in his mouth, the fountaining of natural riches against his palate. As was the case with certain wild flowers, he calls the fruits by their German names rather than by their

English, partly because some of them he's encountered first in Germany, partly because their more sonorous German names are somehow more expressive of their being: *Erdbeeren*, *Johannisbeeren*, *Stachelbeeren*, *Himbeeren* (strawberries, red currants, gooseberries, raspberries). Later, as summer dissolves into early autumn, there are apples, pears and, down in the Rhine valley, plums and peaches, his mother's favourite fruit. They are able to get basketfuls of peaches from villages far to the south of Essen, with black-and-white window-boxed houses and thin-spired churches, and banks of russet-gold woods at their backs. And when you drive home, a pepperminty tang in the air and a haze issuing from cut fields and turned trees, you feel you could arrive at a *real* Dortmund, a *real* Mülheim, a *real* Essen (perhaps as it never quite was, with everyone happily in homes, and trains running and shops where there is food for everyone; with no thin children with sores on their legs and black decay in their teeth, but ones who can afford to keep their dogs and can take them for walks in the park or the *Stadtwald*). All this and more is promised by these afternoons of peaches . . .

Toni and Trude tell him that if you accompany or directly follow gooseberries with a glass of water, you may well fall down dead. In secret he tries this, and survives. His mother says peaches should be peeled, but he disagrees; their furry skins are not only so pretty in themselves, it feels good to rub them against your face. A fruit he doesn't pick or see picked but which appears in the towns, brought from the heathlands to their north, is the *Heidelbeere*, the bilberry, and that perhaps is the most mysteriously lovely of all, both in its colour – its cloudy blue that changes at the touch of a finger – and in the piquancy of its taste, which surprises more than just the tongue, somehow.

In the kitchen Toni and Trude – and their friends, including those men who have dropped in from the Deutsche Polizei – complain increasingly vehemently about Finette. *Die arme Frau Binding* . . . They are angry with Matthias for carrying her and the boy's father about in the car. It's unjust! Matthias tries to shrug it off. If he's asked to, what else can he do? *Donnerwetter!* Toni exclaims irately, banging her clenched hand down upon the kitchen table. *Donnerwetter!* – the worst and, in some circumstances, the best word there is. The boy uses it himself (when alone) on occasions.

His father – who would never use such a word – is also ever more frequently angry. About the Americans. They have got the upper hand over the British now, whatever anyone says, and all his work at Krupp's, all the hard and ambitious work he and his colleagues have been engaged on, will be undone. They might as well not have worked at all.

The Russians are not altogether forgotten in his long, bitter speeches, however. The Allies' meeting with them in April was a disaster: the Russians so clearly wanted to 'bleed' Germany. (And the boy would see blood seeping through the rubble, trickling down the walls of churches, even pouring out through a kind of pulsing wound, in the woods of Bredeney.) They were refusing to release German and Austrian prisoners – almost a million of them they still held! (And among them would be Hannelore's father and Günter's father, pining in the flat, distant east for Essen, not knowing how it was, not knowing that their houses were mere héaps of blackened stones, but not knowing also that their wives and children were well and dreaming of them.)

And then think of all those still trudging into the British Zone from the Eastern, the Russian, one. (As Finette and Achim had done.) When there wasn't enough food to go round *here*! Remember all those people in Hamburg in May who marched through the streets because they hadn't enough to eat . . .

His mother, so big now, so uncharacteristically heavy and awkward in her movements, has become sadder and, unless she and the boy are alone together, stays silent, withdrawn. Finette says she and Achim must move – she wouldn't want to share the house with a *baby*! – but then where can she go to? She'll try to find *somewhere*, however; perhaps the family near Aachen, but she can't really be sure. (Who, the boy realises, have never been talked about since that visit of months ago. So they've remained there, behind their moat, so to speak, on the other side of the drawbridge, amicable but a little melancholy, looking after chickens and rabbits, and every now and again making themselves syrupy waffles.) Besides, Finette continues, she doesn't feel so very well. And rackingly she coughs again. Sometimes the boy's seen her spitting horrible stuff, bloody stuff, into her handkerchief or down the plug-hole of the wash-basin. The boy imagines her away from the house, in unremitting discomfort, alone except for her son, in one of the forlorn encampments on the outskirts of the city, and he can't but feel a pang for her.

And for Achim, too, who loves his mother (no doubt of *that!*), just as the boy loves his.


Dreams are still to be dreaded.

One recurring dream does not take him out of his home. He is down in the *Wintergarten* playing with Debs among the basket chairs, but on a whim decides to go upstairs. For some reason he feels, emanating from the dining-room and from the shut door of his father's study, a warning, and as he ascends the stairs an all too familiar acrid smell comes to him, carried by a cold wind. It is strange, though, to feel the wind on your face indoors, but then, *is* he truly indoors?

By the time he has reached the landing, he knows that his house, like the vast majority of houses in Essen, has been bombed. Instead of doors there are now gashes in burned topless walls; instead of ceiling, sky; and, as he looks through the spaces into the garden, there, blocking out the waxy-flowered magnolia and the great horse-chestnut tree, is a heap of debris containing, among much else, snapped-off chimneys.

Another dream makes him actually enter that fearsome thing, an aeroplane – which is sometimes disguised as an innocuous-seeming booth on the ground. There is a terrifying moment when the plane reveals its true identity and takes off. Above the clouds, the boy finds himself locked in the small contraption with British and – yes – American soldiers, who are at once friendly and menacing. (Americans seem to him a different race, almost a different species, from all other people, bigger, stronger, healthier, the children – he's met several by now – fairer, with golden-hued skins, and loosely easier in their movements.) American soldiers – all wide, cheeky faces and sly mouths – say to him almost casually, 'Let's have some fun, shall we? We can bomb the city below!' The seductive quality of their accents makes the boy think: Is this something I've misunderstood? *Is* it just a case of boyish fun?

He goes over to the plane window where he can see, miles below him, through a parting in the clouds, the towers and avenues of a city. One of the airmen grins conspiratorially and the boy cries out – primarily in appalled indignation at the *reality* behind the proposal, but also because of that second's equivocation on his own part. He'd do anything to prevent the imminent discharge from the aeroplane – even leap from it (as perhaps, in rather different circumstances, Matthias once did), to fall through lakes of clouds, down tunnels of air to death among the (by then) sizzling buildings of the city.


Finette and Achim leave – he is not told for where. Their leaving is not like a departure, even though the boy feels that he'll probably never see them again. There are no affectionate embraces, no thanks, no assurances and promises. As the door closes behind them, the boy understands that, of course, for his father there's no question of leave-taking: he'll be seeing them regularly enough. And he's right: most Saturdays and Sundays his father goes out, and who can doubt in whose company he's spending his time? But when the boy, seeking to please his mother, says bad things about

Finette, he is rebuked. He doesn't know, he's told, what she has endured; he can't, at his age, *begin* to know.

Nevertheless he is very pleased that the door in his room now leads into a room that doesn't contain the woman (and her child) any more. A cot appears in it now, in readiness for his sister. Will it be nice having a sister? (*Schwesterlein, komm, tanz mit mir! Beide Hände reich ich dir . . .*) The two of them might perhaps be like Hänsel and Gretel, devoted and comforting to one another.

Hänsel and Gretel's story never ceases to compel him: perhaps particularly now that the leaves are falling in the deciduous woods, baring the branches, while the Hänsel-and-Gretel forests remain their dark, implacable selves:

> *Hänsel und Gretel verirrten sich im Wald.*
> *Es war schon finster und auch so bitter kalt.*
> *Sie kamen an ein Häuschen von Pfefferkuchen fein:*
> *Wer mag der Herr wohl von diesem Häuschen sein?*

(Hänsel and Gretel lost their way in the wood. It was already dark and also so bitterly cold. They came upon a little house made of sweet gingerbread: Who on earth might the owner of this little house be?)

It was not so very difficult imagining parents who, not having enough to eat themselves, turned their children out into the forest. Hunger is a real enough thing, the boy knows. Nor was it so difficult – with all the unexplained horror about him – for the boy to envisage at the heart of the children's enforced journey a being totally malign, the *Hexe* of the *Kasperltheater*, for there can be no doubting malignity's power, and its servants must often seem amicable enough. He thinks of the British, French and American soldiers he's encountered.

'Ah, you dear children,' (said the *Hexe*) 'what has brought you here? Come in and stop with me, and no harm shall befall you!' and so saying she took them both by the hand, and let them into her cottage. A good meal of milk and pancakes with sugar, apples and nuts was spread on the table, and in the back room were nice little beds, covered with white, where Hänsel and Gretel laid themselves down, and thought themselves in heaven. The old woman had behaved very kindly to them, but in reality she was a wicked old witch who waylaid children and built the bread-house in order to entice them in, but as soon as they were in her power, she killed them, cooked and ate them, and made a great festival of the day.

Nature played a double part in the story: birds ate up the peas Hänsel so cleverly left as a homeward trail, and it was a bird that led the children to the gingerbread house. But – as the boy never stopped remembering – animals and birds were also very helpful to Hänsel and Gretel, and finally assisted them in their return to their father's house.

But what's always troubled the boy troubles him still. When the children arrive home, they find that their step-mother has died, and they are understandably very pleased. But who could consider as a truly happy ending reunion with a man who'd been weak enough – and willing, yes, *willing!* – to go along with her cruel proposals and abandon his only children to the eminently real dangers of a forest? Surely they could never trust him again? The question nags at him and won't let go.


Now, for the first time, the boy appreciates the rolling-round of a year, the death of leaves, the coming-again of frost and snow, St Martin reappearing with his lantern-bearing followers, the closing-in of the days, the putting of a *Schüssel-chen* under the table for St Nicholas to fill with nuts and raisins. Once again the Christ-child will be born, and there'll be the *Tannenbaum* to honour and presents to give and receive.

But before the Christ-child celebrations, there's the birth in his own family. His mother is sent to hospital, to Wuppertal, famous for its overhead suspension railway which has long endeared the place to him. Wuppertal . . . People suffered there almost more than *anywhere* in this region, says his father. 'We' did to that town things which should rank as major crimes . . .

The hospital, the British *Military* Hospital, stands at the top of the hill, and is approached by a steep, bendy road. Ice makes this hard to negotiate, for winter in its severity is setting in again, though people say it will not be quite a repetition of the year before. His mother is in hospital for some weeks; she writes to him every day, however, some-times enclosing with her letter a little present – a book, a Dinky car. (He can read now – it happened almost without his noticing.)

His father goes to visit her a good deal. But Wuppertal is certainly not where he is in the evenings. Though the boy has never found much physical comfort in his father's presence, he is glad – in his mother's absence – of his being there in the house after night has fallen; he likes going to sleep in the knowledge of it. His father obviously doesn't appreciate this, and the boy lies awake . . . waiting, waiting, waiting. When, at the often very late hour he does come back, he is strangely changed, his eyes are glazed over, his speech a little blurry, his movements uncertain.

Toni and Trude – though they never say so to the boy – are angry with his father. It's not hard to see that there's a rift, a wall in the household – his mother, Toni and Trude on one side, and his father and the departed Finette on the other. Somewhere *in* the rift, or *on* the wall, is Matthias. The only other person for whom this partitioned landscape exists is one no longer in the house, who's on the *other* side of another partitioning: Finette's son, Achim. Who has never said or done anything to upset anybody, but has gone his own gentle way always.

Toni sings the boy to sleep on these father-and-mother-less nights, partly perhaps to assuage her own wrath:

> *Weißt du, wieviel Sternlein stehen*
> *an dem blauen Himmelszelt?*
> *Weißt du, wieviel Wolken gehen*
> *weithin über alle Welt?*

The next lines are indeed thought-provoking.

*Gott, der Herr, hat sie gezählet,*
*daß ihm auch nicht eines fehlet*
*an der ganzen großen Zahl,*
*An der ganzen großen Zahl!*

(God, the Lord, has counted them so that not even one is missing, in the whole vast number, in the whole vast number!) Can this, *could* this be true? And how about *people*? What about all those lost Germans in Russia, for example?

One day a tiny wooden train arrives, with a letter saying: 'A present from your brother.' Apparently his parents had changed their minds, and decided on another boy. Though surprised, he is really rather relieved. His mother is quite ill and his father is very worried by this (in addition to his other preoccupations); she and the baby do not return home until just before Christmas. The brother – now installed in Finette and Achim's room – behaves with no awareness of his own role and relationship, which is rather uninteresting of him. He has dark hair – people say that he takes after their mother – and his name is Timothy.

A girl moves into the house to help his mother look after him; nineteen years old, she is called Ursula, and she tells the boy – many times – her dramatic story. And the *way* she tells it, as well as its contents, makes him unfailingly uncomfortable. (That softening between the legs again.) A schoolgirl in Mülheim, she took the last bus home before the Great Disaster – by which she means the bombing of the Möhne Dam. (The boy has been taken to the Möhnesee by

77

his parents, with never a word, though, about the Disaster.) The dam broke, the waters poured through the valley and through Mülheim itself, invading even the mines and underground shelters. Had Ursula caught a later bus she would undoubtedly have been drowned (she says) like so many hundreds of others. He sees her, pretty with her golden, wavy hair, lying under deep swirling water which is rising, rising, to the attic-storeys of Mülheim's hollowed houses.

Everybody becomes happier in the baby's presence. Matthias's first act, every morning now, when he comes round to take Herr Binding to work, is to dash upstairs to Timothy's room and seize him in his arms. Later on, he likes to toss him in the air and deftly catch him. His ravaged face is transfigured by his delight in the baby, which is also, perhaps, a way of apologising to Frau Binding for his driving her husband about with Finette. Toni and Trude – now joined by Ursula – sing lullabies to Timothy suggesting to the older boy a domain of repose so very different from his own troubled sleep.

The boy's father also is very pleased by the baby. He always speaks to it in German, perhaps logically, considering that it's so much in the company of adoring German women. (Consequently the first words Timothy speaks are German ones.) This pleasure apart, his father appears perpetually dissatisfied, broody, uninterested when not dismally preoccupied. He goes out far less often at the weekends now, but this does not mean he spends more time with the boy and the boy's mother, neither of whom he appears to enjoy being with. What has happened to Finette? What is Achim doing now? . . . His father spends much time in his study, but perhaps he isn't always working. Often he comes out with the blankness in his eyes, that almost toy-like way of moving, that strong sourness on his breath, that the boy noticed in that long period of his mother's absence from the house. He can be sleepy at the oddest times, too. Sometimes he falls asleep at mealtimes, sometimes, on drives into the country, his head slumps down and Matthias, noticing this, says that Herr Binding has been very tired recently. Once the boy overhears his mother saying to his father: 'Toni and Trude know *all* about it. How can you think they don't? They've got eyes in their heads.'


His work depresses his father now, when formerly he was excited by it; that's something about his present melancholy that even his mother sympathises with. The Americans have invalidated all the British have done, and all that they've been standing for. And, in addition to that, there's not enough for him to do, he's underoccupied as (were they honest about it!) almost all members of the British Occupation are now.

Yes, his mother agrees, too much time for parties and drink and eyeing the women.

His father would like, he says, another job – with the United Nations. He's bilingual in English and German, one of the very few officially permitted to attend key meetings with Germans without an interpreter. And he has also studied French and Spanish. And then again, he'd like to work in Berlin. Occupation is coming to an end. Life might well be opening out . . . But he doesn't sound as if he really thinks it is – at least, not for himself.

*

During the year they travel a great deal, his father, his mother and himself (the baby stays in Essen, in the care of Ursula), all over western Germany – Nordeney, in the Friesian islands, floating sandbanks in a cold sea where seals can be observed; Hamelin, where he learns about the Pied Piper and buys sugar-rats, and from there pays a second visit to Goslar and the Harz Mountains; the Rhine gorge where he can feast his gaze upon the rock-pinnacling castles and the cataracting vineyards, the river-quays and the wood-filled chasms in the cliffs, seeing a landscape that surpasses those fascinating stories he's been told. Then there's the rich, peaceful Bay-rischer Wald. And down to the Bavarian Alps. They stay in Rottach on Tegernsee. The height of the mountains, the way they raise their snowy heads to defy the clouds, and even, it often seems, the sun itself – never do these cease to make him marvel. Indeed the whole world appears different to the boy after his encounter with their peaks.

In the arguments they have about almost everything, his parents debate the relative merits of sea and mountains. How stupid! As if both aren't inexhaustible. But if he *had* to choose, and he hopes he hasn't, the boy realises that (for once) he must agree with his father. Mountains speak to his heart, as well as to his senses and his mind.

Hamburg, Frankfurt, Munich: these are just as appalling as the cities of the Ruhr. And Berlin, he's always heard, is, if possible, the most ghastly of all. It's hard to know whether seeing those parts of Germany on which the war has left fewer real scars makes these cities the more or the less hard to bear. In them now you see men and women labouring away at the rubble, clearing it (almost like birds pecking at huge, fallen trunks), so that new homes can arise in its stead. It's a doomed task, isn't it? But his father says that with the Germans' will and their ability to work hard, the towns can soon – all of them, even Berlin – stand proudly up again.

In Berchtesgaden it's possible to take a trip up a mountain to where once stood the home of the wickedest man there's ever been. His parents emphatically do *not* want to go there – they are agreed on that point anyway. Instead they visit a little house in the village where cuckoo clocks are both made and sold. The workshop smells deliciously of sweet wood, and the boy is bought a clock. 'It can be like a companion to you,' they say.

For his dearest companion is gone. One evening Toni took a walk and decided – as she sometimes did – that Debs should accompany her. She returned late, far, far later than expected, crying as he'd never imagined the stalwart Toni would cry. She wouldn't see him, only his mother. Later he's told that Debs slipped the leash, and has run away. Perhaps he joined those children who'd brought him to the house the winter before last. Perhaps. But the boy knows that this isn't what happened, that Debs is no more, was killed – and before Toni's eyes. Things can be like that. Existence means sadnesses so inexorable that they can't be wept over, though silently – by day and at night – his *heart* weeps and weeps.


Berlin, Berlin, Berlin . . . For the first time, something happening in Germany preoccupies his mother even more than his father (who seems beset anyway by so many worries, inexpressible, it would appear, to his own household). Almost every day there seems to be fresh grounds for alarm and talk from this city about which he has heard so much already – from his parents, from Finette, from other members of the British community in the Ruhr – the city which, his father says, is the *true* capital of Germany, just as London is the capital of England. What a blessing we aren't living there, his mother interrupts, and who knows how its present troubles will end?

The boy finds it very hard to make out what has been – and indeed still is – happening over there. First, in the spring, the Russians tried to block trains and cars taking people (which might so well have included his family and himself) into Berlin. Then their grip on the city tightened, and by summer people were in danger of their supplies of food running out – they were hungrier, a great deal hungrier, it would seem, than even the Germans back here in Westfalen. And so started the airlift, continuing now. The airlift is a good thing, indeed a wonderful thing, he's told, a plane taking off from Hanover and landing at first every four minutes, then later (now!) every two, bringing the suffering citizens food to carry them through the next weeks – no, the next *days*. But 'airlifts', to the boy, does not *sound* good because it makes him think of the terror and pain that has been brought directly from the air on to the country he is living in – and on to others too, even England, he now understands. One hot day, when they're in Bavaria – the sun silvering Tegernsee, the mountain-peaks rising against a cloudless baked-blue sky – they hear that Russians have turned guns on Germans in Berlin who've been publicly protesting at the situation. Is that how wars begin? the boy wonders, for no one has explained to him how this actually occurs, let alone how the particular war between his own two countries (as he now thinks of them) began. And no sooner has he framed the question to himself than his mother says aloud, to his father: 'Is this how wars begin?'

That night his father is so exceedingly strange (and in that way by now not exactly unfamiliar) that the boy's mother takes refuge in his room all night. When his father is strange, he often sings German songs tunelessly to himself:

> *Alle Tage ist kein Sonntag,*
> *Alle Tage ist kein Wein*

(Not every day is a Sunday, not every day is there wine.)

The lines are as frightening as the news, and, oddly, in the same way.

# Four

Trude's husband has come back from Russia, and she has left Tirpitzstraße 49 to make a home for him again. (And Toni, happy at Trude's good fortune, is plainly always thinking: And *my* husband? What's happened to *him*? Surely I've been right supposing all this time that he's one of the hundreds of thousands for whom 'missing' means 'dead'?)

Trude pays frequent visits to their house, however (where her work has been taken over by Ursula), and her face shows none of the joy that suffused it when she heard the news of her husband's imminent return. She looks pinched and anxious and talks to Toni and Matthias – and to the boy's mother – in a low troubled voice; when she thinks the boy can hear her, she stops. But he *has* heard her – well at least enough. She'd expected her man to be thin, weakened, yes, exhausted, bewildered. But she'd never thought he wouldn't be himself. But he's not the man who left Germany, in fact he's more of a shadow than a man. All day long he just sits and sits on the edge of the bed, his eyes staring, unfocused, beyond the objects around him. It's as if the world wasn't real to him (and perhaps it isn't, thinks the boy, remembering

Matthias's home), as if he's in some other one. At night he can't sleep, but by day he appears scarcely awake, like someone still dreaming bad dreams.

Trude feels sorry for him, but she can't help feeling sorry for herself too; she tries her hardest to think of things to arouse his attention, to make him want to eat or move about. But she feels sorriest of all for Günter. He'd been looking forward so much to his father's return, but now he resents it. He's frightened by this person who hardly notices he's there, who looks through him . . .

Günter accompanies his mother to Tirpitzstraße occasionally, and the boy notices a certain dejection in the way he holds himself or answers questions. He'd like to say something to cheer him up but can think of nothing suitable, nothing that wouldn't suggest he's been eavesdropping. Besides, Günter is a little bored by him, doesn't want to be bothered with little kids any more. The days of 'Wir sind böse Männer' seem long past.


With so much news to be heard these days about Russia, America and China, about Britain, France and the Zones of Germany, about Berlin (almost a country on its own, so complicated seem its problems), the boy wants to know more precisely where the various countries are, where they stand in relation to each other, their shapes, their sizes, their borders. He has now seen many borders – the Dutch one, the Belgian one, the Austrian one, the Czechoslovakian one. Britain had the sea for a border. And Germany had borders within itself – between the Zones. These borders involve changes of soldiers, though there's something in the faces of *all* soldiers that makes them, for him, much the same as each other.

His father promises him an atlas. It will have to be ordered from England. The best atlas is Roderick Meiklejohn's School Atlas, and it will tell him all he wants to know.

His father only goes away by himself occasionally now: the very names of Finette and Achim aren't spoken any more (or if they are, the boy doesn't hear them). It's as if the baby, installed in the mother and son's old room, has vanquished them. But he knows his father goes on thinking about Finette.

He himself thinks more about Achim (*let* Finette be vanquished!). Achim may have had to decline his offer of toys, but he didn't decline his company. He was preferable by far to Philip or Elspeth. And now like poor Debs he's disappeared into a Nowhere.

The boy's father spends even more of his time shut up in his study. He writes long letters to England, and awaits the replies eagerly, almost nervously. He clearly wants these to comfort him, but he is also a little afraid of what they're going to say.

Often when they go out for their walks, his mother takes the baby in his pram. The air in the Ruhr is so dirty, she complains, look at the soot and little splinters of coal on the coverlet. His mother – far livelier these days – wins many compliments: German and English alike bend over the pram to smile at the sleeping child or to run an admiring finger down the dark wispy hair on his head. One day, however, something very different takes place. They're making their way towards the Balderneysee, when out of nowhere a wiry-looking German boy, with tufty fair hair and a spot-pocked face, appears. With a look of real committed hatred on his face he leans over and spits in the baby's face. The mother stops the pram quickly – indeed she has to, the boy has blocked the pavement. A quick hostile glance up, and once again he spits right into the baby's eyes. The boy expects his mother to be furious at this insult to her new son, but she isn't; she looks regretful and takes hold of the German boy's arm. 'Little English swine,' he says, and tries yet another expectoration, but the boy's mother has quite a firm grip, and perhaps his spasm of resentment has passed (for truly the boy seemed to be spitting not just with his mouth but with the whole of himself, with his rancorous soul). 'Why do you want to do that?' the boy's mother asks in her sing-song German. 'A baby can't have done you any harm.'

The boy snarls at her, and frees himself from the English-woman (who's loosened her hold anyway). Then he takes to his heels and runs, back in the direction of the city, his desert-home.

'That's the very first time,' the boy's mother says as they continue their walk, 'that I've ever encountered any anger that we're here.'

(But why exactly *are* we here? The boy has not desisted from his questions. Has, in fact, elaborated them. And dismisses too pat or condescending an evasion.)

'It was horrid of him to spit at Timothy, wasn't it?'

His mother doesn't exactly agree with this. 'It's how he feels. I might feel the same in his position. I don't blame him, I *can't* blame him. We don't know what he's been through.'

But perhaps I do, thinks the boy, flames and collapsing buildings, and underground shelters where people sometimes turned crazy because of the hellish noises overhead, because of their fear within. (Yes, all this he knows now.) And no home to live in; not for him the rose-patterned walls and carpeted floors of Tirpitzstraße 49. Compared with what he's been through (yes, his mother's right), what did a few malevolent drops of spittle on a baby's head signify?

A German couldn't, perhaps shouldn't, like the British to be walking about as if they were in charge of everything. (Though they *were* in charge of everything – here at any rate.) He didn't like all these walls, all these borders between people, just as he didn't like cages for animals.

That was one thing wrong with the atlas, though in other ways it's a more wonderful book even than he'd dared to hope, showing him countries and seas that he'd never imagined existed. Germany appears as a large, clean, yellow splodge, without any sign of a British, a French, an American or a Russian Zone; neither is there any evidence that Berlin's a divided city with one part blocked so that it's an island, having to have food dropped on it every second minute by air. Atlas-makers can't be expected to keep up with the news, his father explains, it takes time to produce a book . . . And there's another thing, too: the maps don't show you which are the whole cities and which the broken ones. Isn't it wrong that Hamburg, Osnabrück, Hannover, Cologne, Essen should have no marks that distinguish them from Heidelberg or all those towns in England where friends or relations of his parents live, innocent of ruins? He expects all books to tell the truth.

The atlas doesn't show where God lives either. God the crimson-robed, golden-crowned *Kasperltheater* king? God has now entered his parents' conversation, and again they are disagreeing about things; again he himself is involved, though not addressed; again there's a dividing line, a sort of wall.

The boy thinks about their holiday down in Bavaria. They'd gone to visit the Passion Theatre at Oberammergau. In it and in the villages nearby, set amid lush, flower-filled meadows and overlooked by the great mountains, you saw houses with scenes painted in bright colours between the eaves. The boy's father told him that these, for the most part, were episodes from the life of Jesus Christ, God's son, and in Oberammergau itself he was actually introduced to Jesus Christ and to Joseph his earthly father, and to Mary Magdalene, his great friend, and to Judas Iscariot, who'd sold him to the enemy. After only a few minutes he understood – as obviously also had been the case with St Martin, clip-clopping through Bredeney – that these people were *pretending* to be those famous ones of long ago. Moreover you could see images of Jesus when he was dead, nailed to the cross, with great wounds on his body – they were everywhere in Bavaria, at the beginning, at the meeting-point, at the end of paths, carved out of wood and brightly painted, placed in little wayside shrines and honoured with bunches of flowers.

'Oberammergau and all the shrines and churches of Bavaria,' says his father, 'provide yet further examples of the worldwide appeal of the Roman Catholic Church. Every kind of person, from a mountain villager to a great and clever man like Konrad Adenauer, can accept it and find strength and comfort in it.' In Essen Dr Ahlens, Toni and Trude do (Ursula goes to the Evangelische Kirche). 'I repeat, it's the one church that war-torn Europe knows, from Ireland to Poland, from Holland to the tip of Italy.'

'Yes, and what did the Church do to stop the war?' objects his mother. 'You ask your Finette and learn how little it did to help her people!' (For once his mother sounds as if she's *siding* with Finette against something, is feeling for her.) 'And, worse – what did God do?' she says, one day, when she thinks the boy isn't listening.

The letters his father writes when shut up in his study are to a clergyman in the Roman Catholic Church (a man of God, like the boy's grandfather, only, in important ways, *not* like him). The clergyman's name is Fr Martindale, and the replies he sends are the most wonderful letters his father has ever received – full of such understanding and hope.

All the same, his father's strange ways do not cease. Sometimes, when he's at his strangest, he says that he has to 'change his faith'.

His mother says in a quiet, cold voice: 'Change it if you want to, but I won't have my sons brought up in it.'

'You don't understand! You understand nothing!'

'I do, I was educated at a convent, and I was very fond of the sisters there.'

' "Fond of the sisters",' echoes his father sarcastically.

'But that doesn't mean *I* believe what *they* believe. Nor do I want to. Nor do I want my sons to.'

Silence. His father's eyes are bloodshot and bulging.

'What was God doing in Wuppertal?' his mother says. Wuppertal, where his brother was born!

'In *Wuppertal*!'

'Yes, when people were set on fire by phosphorus bombs and rushed into the River Wupper to put themselves out. And drowned!'

His father sighs. 'Finette, at least, would approach the subject more *intelligently*,' he said, 'and, as you pointed out, she's actually experienced suffering. Which *you* have not!'

'Mummy,' the boy inquires, remembering this newest example of the horror that literally fell down upon Westfalen, 'the Germans don't hate us, do they?'

She smiles gently at him. 'Look at Toni and Ursula. Do *they* hate you?'

'No. But that German boy who spat?'

'As I told you, I haven't met anyone else who's acted as he did, and maybe he had a special reason, some particular thing that had gone wrong for him. When the British and Americans came into the Ruhr, even before the war ended, everyone here was delighted. They were as pleased as we were that the whole thing was over. They knew we meant peace.'

'Even after we'd dropped all those bombs on them?'

'Paul, you must try to stop thinking so much about the bombs!'

'If the German boy who spat at Timothy had known I was a bit German myself, do you think he'd have been different?'

He's vexed his mother by his questions. 'I really don't know. Shall we talk about something else?'

His mother, who has held back from most other British people in Essen, has a real friend now, someone who's been a teacher like herself. She is an almost daily visitor to Tirpitz-straße 49. Her name is Mrs Preuss.

All during the war, all during the years of the bombs upon the Ruhr, Mrs Preuss – who is as English as the boy's own mother – lived in Germany. She was married to a German, the father of her three children. Even before the war her English relations begged her to leave Germany; she wouldn't. Those she loved came before any other consideration: their people were her people now. The German authorities looked on her position with a certain suspicion, which increased after her husband was killed during all the fighting in Russia. But she was legally German, and German too were her two sons and her daughter. Throughout the rain of fire on the German towns, she lived a grim and lonely life, but they survived.

The war came to its end. (Just how, the boy still wonders, exactly how, does a war do this? Is there a final cry going up from the remaining inhabitants of the battered cities, a '*Please*, don't do this to us any more!'?) But Mrs Preuss's problems did not. She wanted to be recognised by the occupiers, and treated by them as one of their number. She fought a long, bitter battle with the authorities, an unpleasant affair. 'It was as if, Muriel,' she remarked to the boy's mother, 'I had been guilty of all the German crimes.' (German crimes! what were these?) Eventually, however, she was granted the status she wanted, partly through the friendship of a senior officer in the British Army.

This man visited her house on the outskirts of Essen, often bringing with him a younger Englishman, a relation of his, serving in the Army under him. The young man liked to play with the three children who'd had so rough a time, not quite belonging anywhere, suffering on *both* sides, as it were.

One summer afternoon this young soldier organised a game. They all pretended there was a battle on again: the visitor pointed his gun at Mrs Preuss's little girl – and shot her dead.

Mrs Preuss looks like a bright little bird, a robin or a wren. She couldn't be defeated, even by this tragedy, and absolutely forbade the court-martialling of the soldier. One morning not long afterwards her elder son, Martin, woke up unable to speak.

He can speak a little now. The boy meets him from time to time; he'll roll his head from side to side, and his eyes have a vacant expression.

Like Trude's husband's, perhaps.

What did this tale tell you? That God the crown-wearing king let the unfairest things happen. That even outside the sphere of war and bombardment, suffering and death struck the innocent. Also it told you that – even in play, in a summer garden – guns and battles were against life.

'Muriel,' Mrs Preuss asks his mother many a time, 'do *you* think I behaved wrongly to stay in Germany as I did? Was it bad of me? Have I been punished for doing so?'

There are too many difficult things to think about, but one thing is certain: war and anything to do with it is entirely detestable, entirely wicked. How fed up he is by people's implications that it's odd of him ('an odd child') to be so preoccupied with the bombing, to have taken against soldiers so, not being able to endure even a toy tank or a toy gun! How fed up too he is with silly Philip's continual declaration that he wants to be a soldier! These declarations are made the more insistently because he knows they'll upset the boy. And if he's too upset, he may get into trouble ('highly strung', 'overwrought').

One morning he says to himself: Today if Philip says yet again that he wants to be a soldier, I shall kick him. Morning lessons begin – the reading exercises that he enjoys, the number lessons that he does not, and then the break. Maybe he turns the conversation so that Philip can make his detestable remark. 'Of course I want to be a soldier,' he – predictably – says. 'I shall be a soldier and fight the Germans if they're bad again!'

The boy finds a strength, a cruel strength, to raise his foot, with a suddenness that takes the two of them by surprise, to kick Philip hard between the legs.

There's a scream, followed by tears; his mother and Philip's mother appear in the room. The boy, shamefully, attempts denial, which he then changes to sullen admission. He won't say he's sorry.

He's sent to his room, and even there he doesn't know his feelings about what he's done. He knows it's contradictory to have used violence because you dislike violence, but then . . . Philip should be made to understand the wrongness, the stupidity of his ambition, his views.

The terrible thing is that the kick is related to all that he fears and is set against. He wanted to hurt Philip but he didn't like doing so, and even more dislikes *having done so*. The howl of pain, the blubbery puffiness of Philip's face – to have brought about this reduction of someone, even for a few minutes, that was bad. He'll try not to do it again.

He's fallen ill, with measles. The room is made dark, but it hardly matters, there's such pain in his head, with lights shooting through it. His fever's high. At the foot of his bed he sees the *Kasperltheater*, and all the puppets jiggling about in it, banging their papier mâché heads against one another. The king who is God reels about, the queen weeps, the peasant-boy sags, Gretchen is perhaps dead, Kasperle (as is his wont) frets and fumes but can do absolutely nothing. There, in the blackness of his sick-room, the witch and the ghost are triumphant. He can see the evil glare of the twisted old woman's one open eye, and as for the ghost, being all white, these conditions are its own realm. It will see to it that however hard they work – the *Trümmerfrauen* (rubble-women) restoring the cities, making them *whole* again –there'll always be empty chaos somewhere . . .

Günter appears. *Wir sind böse Männer.* Breaking every law, he's entered the house and released the blinds and there's light and the puppets jig back again, into a sort of order, appropriately, with the witch and the ghost subjugated, in their places at the back. And Günter, his former, not his present miserable self, winks at him in triumph and – and the room turns dark again.

Even little children can die – think how many did, not so long ago, right here in Essen. He wishes he'd been completely good. He must be kind to Finette when next he sees her. But he doesn't know where she is. And Achim – he wants to see Achim . . .

In his convalescence his parents take it in turns to read to him – in particular *The Wind in the Willows* by Kenneth Grahame. It's the first long book, the first one that resembles a grown-ups' book, that has been offered to him. He is enthralled by it, by all the secret lives of the creatures of wood and field and riverbank, revealed in their everyday joys and sorrows, activities and dangers. Even more than the preposterous conceit and misadventures of Toad does this aspect of the book appeal to him: its articulation of the thoughts and feelings of the shy, vulnerable and inarticulate – of moles, water-rats, badgers and otters.

In most of the other stories he's been read – for example, the tales of the Brothers Grimm, by Trude – you encounter animals as pointers on a path: they aren't as important in themselves as the human beings they help. But here, in this British story, the animals are not only important, you're asked to *become* them. You treat them as you would a human being.

(A barrier has been removed, a border crossed, an occupation zone penetrated and freed.)

There's one chapter in the book his parents say is too old for him, but at his insistence they eventually capitulate and read it to him. It's called 'The Piper at the Gates of Dawn'.

The otter's son has gone missing, and when he's tracked down, it's to a little river-island, where a goat-footed being plays music.

Slowly, but with no doubt or hesitation whatever, and in something of a solemn expectancy, the two animals passed through the broken, tumultuous water and moored their boat at the flowery margin of the island. In silence they landed, and pushed through the blossom and scented herbage and undergrowth that led up to the level ground, till they stood on a little lawn of a marvellous green, set round with Nature's own orchard-trees – crab-apple, wild cherry and sloe.

'This is the place of my song-dream, the place the music played to me,' whispered the Rat, as if in a trance. 'Here, in this holy place, here if anywhere surely we shall find Him.'

Then suddenly the Mole felt a great Awe fall upon him, an aura that turned his muscles to water, bowed his head, and rooted his feet to the ground. It was no panic terror – indeed he felt wonderfully at peace and happy – but it was an awe that smote and held him and, without seeing, he knew it could only mean that some august Presence was very, very near.

Isn't that what the boy has felt (more faintly, perhaps) by the deserted, railed-off menagerie in Bredeney wood? Isn't that what all human beings and animals must be able to feel at some point in their lives, though words may evade them? Isn't that what war and the emotions of war, what all aggressive acts and thoughts undermine or keep at bay? Wouldn't that Awe, that Presence, be worth striving to find when he was a bit older, and able to decide things for himself, when he could devote himself to discovering what forces lie behind and animate the rustlings, bayings, scratchings and singing of an infinitely various creature-world?

But will he be in England by then (for already the continuing trouble in Berlin is making his parents think about going back there) or still in Germany? (To which, he learns, independence is coming!) Will he be a German boy in England or an English boy in Germany? Or an English boy in England. Or a German boy in Germany?

Or will he not be quite any of these?

When he does his lessons, he feels English. When he goes to sleep at night, when he wakes up in the morning, when he receives feelings of joy or of despair from the tangible world about him, then he feels German. There are huge areas, however, between these two states – how will they be filled?

He's started to draw pictures. Some are of the most beautiful city he can imagine (he gives it the name of Lemontine), which looks like Aladdin's Peking, and like other Chinese cities as picture-books have shown them: tiled roofs, pagodas, painted walls, little gardens. But he also finds a compulsion to draw the most horrible picture in his power.

It's of a group of evil witches and under it – under their grotesque bodies topped by snarling heads – he writes the name of their crime:

NOT TELLIG THE TRUOTH

For there have been so many truths he's not been told: about the bombing, about the war, about why and how they are living in Germany. About his father and mother and their feelings for each other, about his father and Finette, about Finette and Achim and their lives before they moved into Tirpitzstraße 49.

He's sensed that there isn't even truth in his home. It should be German but is lived in by English people. It should contain a family who are united by their relationships, not one where both parents prefer to be with people of a different nationality from themselves.


On a drive through the Rhineland bound homewards for Essen, they stop at a small town where there's a fair. It's evening; the merry-go-round with its leaping caparisoned wooden horses is shining against the dusk. The boy asks if he can have a ride on it. Oompah music pounds out jollily into the unknown evening town, and the horses rise and fall as the roundabout turns. In front of him, next to him, sharing the fun, are German children, but on the two horses directly behind him sit two small boys speaking a language that is neither English nor German – they call out something to him, but he can't reply. They call out again, but anyway the speed is increasing: he is too caught up in movement and hurdy-gurdy melody to be obliged to reply. They're in the French Zone, he remembers, so the boys at his back are most probably French themselves. At its fastest the merry-go-round makes clear viewing of the world impossible: his mother and father and Matthias are turned into quick-passing blurs, and for these moments he is content that this is so. Completely at one with other children of differing nationalities, united all of them by a common and time-hallowed delight – isn't this how things should be? Isn't the thumping tune expressive of a TRUOTH at least as comprehensive and full as any his parents and their friends have expounded to him?

It's a real pity when music and roundabout slow towards a halt, and horses cease to bob up and down, and you have to step out into the dull, darkening fairground and into your usual role.


The decision has been taken. Their life in Essen is drawing to its close. Matthias drives them through those pleasant tree-lined roads of Bredeney into that downtown wildness of ruins – all over which work is now being done towards rebuilding – and so to the station. Matthias is making it his business to be as blithe as possible: anyway the good Herr Binding has promised to look out for a job for him in England, not probably as his own driver, but maybe in some car company or other. Ursula is going with the family, to help Frau Binding to look after the baby (who is really a baby no longer because he can walk and say words). To imagine himself again the little child who arrived at Essen station totally ignorant of what had happened in this country, of the breaking of its buildings and the humbling of its people, is as hard as to imagine himself Timothy's innocent age again.

On the platform Toni cries and cries; she cries as she embraces each member of the family, she cries as they, together with Ursula, climb into the railway compartment they've reserved, her good-humoured, plump face all blotchy and swollen with her sadness. And as the train slowly chugs away from the station, she is, the boy sees, still crying, even as she goes on waving at them.

Perhaps it's only now that the boy realises how much and how deeply he's loved her. For a good half of his life, she has been a daily presence, dependable, unsparing, affectionate, not subject to the moods and caprices of his mother or the melancholia of his father, not afraid to rebuke him when he's been selfish or ungrateful, but never grudge-holding, a constant source of warmth and desire for life.

And he's not told her any of this. But, perhaps he'd been wrong to think nobody in Germany had spoken the TRUOTH, for Toni acknowledged only one: kind and direct dealings between people, whatever or whoever they were.


It is impossible, no matter how sad he is within, not to be delighted by Holland. His father says that this country suffered abominably during the war, but to a child who's known the Ruhr as his own particular territory, its scars are not conspicuous: the land exudes peace – an active, indeed busy kind – rather than the distant, dreamy one such as hangs about thick woods and the horizon's hills. It also exudes

**101**

something else that he hasn't seen anywhere before – a contentment with the business of ordinary human living. The water that flows along the dyked canals and encircles little villages and farmsteads and houses glints in the sun; the sails of windmills turn round in the light breeze. All houses, all streets seem so scrubbed and neat and fresh-painted; cheerful people on bicycles are visible everywhere, proclaiming to those who see them from the moving train that yes, going about your humdrum work *can* be enjoyable, life isn't only taxing, saddening, uncertain journeys. On some roofs are flat, round nests: his mother tells him that these are for storks. On stations, and sitting in railway trains, are women in long and voluminous black dresses and white, flap-eared, laced caps, and the youths bustling on the platforms wear baggy blue trousers. They too wear caps, but peaked ones, black or blue. Holland cannot last long enough for the boy. It suggests as possible things that the Ruhr cities had suggested were *im*possible.

They embark at the Hook of Holland: their boat is called the *Oranje-Nassau*. On the other side of the sullen-coloured, choppy sea lies his own country, a new country. The North Sea seems a far greater, more separating boundary than any guarded line.

They walk from one deck to another, down the stairs towards their cabins, his father and mother together, he himself behind them, and Ursula and his brother bringing up the rear. The boy doesn't know whether he's feeling sad or excited. Ahead there's school to go to, other children to play and make friends with. But there's also the grown-up English. In Essen he hadn't liked a single one of them. From the Germans he received warmth, kindly attention, introductions through song and story and games to a world in which his imagination could, with pleasure, dwell. From the English – not counting his parents or Mrs Preuss – a cold, judging, ever-ready contempt came to him, a hardness, a total refusal of imaginative sympathy.

His parents have reached the bottom of the stairs. His father turns to his mother and says:

'I must tell you something: I haven't found myself able to until this minute. Yesterday I got a letter.'

'Yes?'

'It had bad news in it.'

'Yes?'

'Finette is dead.'

The words will never altogether fade away, spoken so unexpectedly and with such pain in this place of transit.

How many seconds, minutes, later does the boy blurt out: 'Mummy, aren't you *pleased*? Aren't you very *pleased* that she's dead?'

There's agony, anger and the dislike for him he's never quite able to shed on his father's face. His mother swings round fiercely to confront him. 'Paul,' she says, 'I never want to hear you say such a dreadful, dreadful thing again.'

She turns to her husband. 'Achim!' she exclaims. 'Whatever's going to become of Achim?'

And at the mention of Achim's name, Achim whose room had had a connecting door into his own, who had once been part of the same household as himself, a desolation sweeps through his whole body, and the death of the dark beautiful woman whom he never liked becomes real to him. Never again will he see her, will *anyone* see her. 'Never again'! What frightening words.

The England of 1949 is waiting for him, on disembarkation from the Dutch boat, and perhaps he thinks that all its demands, present and future, will turn him into an English boy, an English man, after all. He doesn't (or does he?) understand that he will carry these years in fractured Germany about with him always (just as, until his dying days, his father will carry in his wallet Finette's picture and letters), and that they will influence – maybe condition – just about everything for him.

# PART TWO

# Berlin

# One

Forty years later another Dutch boat (the *Königin Beatrix*) and another wintry crossing of the North Sea, only this time the other way about, from Harwich to the Hook of Holland. And again a train journey through the Netherlands, but now into Germany not out of it, to her former heart: Berlin. Forty years earlier Berlin frightened, repelled; now, in less than two months, she's become a magnet. And one of the many she's drawing to herself is a traveller who has suddenly come to feel close to that small boy of 1949, who sailed on a Dutch boat and worried about the future.

This traveller is not far off his forty-seventh birthday (a fact that he finds hard to adjust to, though his life has of late come to seem to him long in its duration); he's 'of no fixed abode', without dependants and a regular job. He still holds a British passport, but he has presented it so many times and at so many frontiers that he regards it as more of a ticket and a proof of identity than as a document testifying to membership of a nation. Perhaps that's how he wants things. He's not sure. Will Berlin have something to teach him in this respect?

*

He comes upon it almost abruptly, as a result of following purposefully moving people down one of the broader paths through the wood. And no sooner has he seen it, beyond the parting in the bare trees (the profusion and brilliance of the graffiti unable to redeem its essential bleakness) than he hears it. It is more extensively audible than visible, and its sound is quite unlike any he's ever heard before. Now they've all but reached it, people quicken their pace. It is as if they are afraid they might arrive there just too late.

At the foot of the Wall, and also – these fewer in number – clinging to its surface, the makers of the sound are revealed. The traveller finds a host with hammers, tap-tapping, chip-chipping, entirely absorbed in its task. A host informed by obvious patience and determination, but also by urgency. Time – which has not shown itself kind – might betray them again.

Between the end of the wood and the Wall runs a path wider than any that lead into it, sandy and puddle-strewn on this rainy day. Those who are making their way along it are mostly looking for where best to fit themselves in among the workers on the Wall. The very old, and the very young, also, are there. Most of them are German; a fair number of the young men – to judge by their greyish-blue stone-washed jeans, dark anoraks and ankle boots – come from the Wall's other side.

Is the Wall under attack?

Not exactly; there's no ferocity behind these hammers.

Is it being punished? Huge holes have been made.

No, violence is not being done. Breaking off chunks requires precision, care.

Is it then being mocked?

No, for all their smiles, people are entirely serious here.

It's almost as if – at last – the Wall were wanted.

To the traveller's right is the waste-ground of the Potsdamer Platz. To the left stand the Brandenburger Tor and the Reichstag. It is to the left that he turns, to find himself amongst an even greater throng.

Graffiti seem to the traveller like the traditional songs of childhood: even while being allusive and suggestive, each slogan has a completeness, is a small world unto itself.

There are some, of course, which are direct and unambiguous: MADE IN DDR, and MAUER ZU VERKAUFEN (Wall for sale). NO EUROPE WITHOUT BERLIN proclaims another. (It appears in German too: KEIN EUROPA OHNE BERLIN.) Great crude lettering testifies to many a cause: NEUES FORUM, FREEDOM FOR TRANSYLVANIA, LITHUANIA FREE, LATVIJU!, AFGHANISTAN LEGT, and (repeating what workers with their hammers announce in a more practical way) DEUTSCHE JUGEND FÜR DEUTSCHE EINHEIT (German youth for German unity).

But here's a more teasing one:

POUR CERTAIN LA LIBERTÉ EST UNE RÊVE.

Did its writer, wonders the traveller, mean that liberty is something we all desire, we all *dream* of, or did he believe that it had no more substance than a dream?

109

The Nightmare was the Wall before 9 November, the Wall as the traveller remembered it on his first visit to Berlin twenty-two years before. It was a physical realisation of fears and hatreds. Part of it was made up of still ruined ('broken') houses, souvenirs of harassment from the air (for the quarters between the Russian and the other sectors had not been much rebuilt). It had seemed only appropriate to the traveller, looking at this symbol of division, that forms such as had darkened his childhood should have gone into its making.

### WE ARE ALL LIKE FLIES.

The dauber was probably thinking of those many who'd met their deaths trying to escape over the Wall between 1961 and this year, swatted by bullets like insects by rolled-up newspapers. But then there was the echo of Shakespeare's *King Lear:* 'As flies to wanton boys are we to the gods, They kill us for their sport.'

If you could watch a speeded-up film of all that's taken place in Berlin since 1918, wouldn't it be all too easy to imagine some sadistic force gratifying itself at humans' expense: from the bloody failure of the Spartacists to the bitter farce of gross inflation, from the obscene cruelties of the Kristallnacht to the inferno of Berlin under day-and-night bombardment, from the ruthless march-in of the Russians to the erection of the Wall itself? And sharers in suffering should have been brought together, not forcibly kept apart.

Here, though, was another interpretation of life, of events:

> GOD LOVES US ALL
> BUT WHY THIS WALL (*sic*)
> TAKE IT DOWN
> PEACE FOR ALL.

Those two old men up there must share this writer's beliefs. They're nailing Christmas wreaths to the top of the Wall. Little mottoes of good will flutter from the leaves and scarlet flowers.

The slogan that has the greatest effect on the traveller that day is, however, this one:

> I HAVE SEEN THE FUTURE AND IT RUNS THROUGH
> THE HEART OF BERLIN.

This, he knows, will sing itself repeatedly throughout his Berlin days – and throughout the nights too, when past scenes translated or revisited by his older self also point towards the years ahead, for himself, for his society.

Moving on towards the Brandenburger Tor he sees tables spread with leaflets and staffed by young men and women valiantly trying to pretend they're not feeling the cold. He takes some hand-outs; one is an English translation of their organisation's declaration. It's called Project Meiga Experiment für eine humane Erde (Experiment for a Humane Earth) and the logo terminates in the word 'Sexpeace'.

The wall is crumbling. It was the symbol of a battle

between two systems. We thank all friends from the German Democratic Republic and the Federal Republic of Germany who have now left this struggle behind. In our country a joy has arisen in which we all partake. This joy comes from the feeling of a universal human sense of belonging, rather than from the triumph of victory. No one has won yet, for we will only have won when all systems and all walls have been overcome. No one will be able to find the human happiness that we all long for, by changing from one system to another. The question of human freedom lies outside all existing political systems. It has not been resolved on either side. The West has more glitter, more drive and more riches but it too has no real answers to the hopes with which hundreds of thousands are coming to us after having lived behind walls for so long.

At this moment we wish to thank the Neues Forum of the GDR for their earnest reflections.

We have always built walls. We have built them to protect ourselves. They have been built around peoples, around political systems and around religious beliefs. They have even been built around human concerns: around Eros, love and partnership. Every bit of insight, every bit of truth and every bit of love that could be found in this difficult world was immediately protected by a wall, an ideology or a law. To the outside world this was a demonstration of strength, but at the same time it was always a protection against fear. But the freedom we all long for is without fear. It is founded on an understanding and solidarity common to all, on friendship and truth between peoples who no longer have to build walls to protect themselves. Wherever walls are needed to protect truth, humaneness and free-dom against the world, we have a contradiction. For human beings can only be truly free in this world if they no longer need barriers and walls.

For the time being the traveller reads no more; already, taking in these sentences on his chilly walk, he feels curiously touched by them, almost as if the pony-tailed, bearded students, with their conscious gentleness, had written them with him in mind.

In the Germany of his early childhood there'd been walls everywhere, between occupier and occupied, within the occupiers and within the occupied. A small boy, while puzzled by them, can also be aware of them; defiance of their existence has to mean – almost above everything else – a putting-up of walls round oneself. It was a habit he took back to England with him, though he was a reluctant builder and an erratic one. But all too soon he learned how to protect his fiercest convictions, his most intimate passions and dreams. For a good part of his life he persuaded himself that things would have been different elsewhere; except in particulars there was no reason to suppose that would have been the case. But it was less frightening believing this than admitting the validity of other explanations of these walls.

Would the authors of this propaganda sheet think that he has accepted, or even colluded in, the erection of walls round 'Eros, love and partnership' in his life? Berlin might show him how he has.


He feels he has become someone whose home is the journey, who finds his security on ships, trains, long-distance coaches, at passport controls and Customs, on gangways and quays and at railway stations. An impersonal hotel or hostel room, though he may dislike or resent it, has become a norm for him. Means of forward motion are like fixed points in his life. He's come to prefer anonymous crowds and the heterogeneousness of fellow-passengers to neighbours – assuming he's ever really had any.

He wonders how many other people – of the thousands in sight now – resemble him in this respect.

For now he's reached one of those barriers of which his life seems so made up, but this is perhaps the most famous one in the world.

It is the point of entrance on foot into East Berlin from West Berlin, the right side (approaching things from the Western point of view) of the Brandenburger Tor. Only yesterday the great gate was opened, though the likelihood of this was acknowledged, and treated as a marvellous fact, for some days beforehand. Ahead there is a queue of immense proportions – in fact it's impossible from this angle to see where it begins. It moves only very slowly, so slowly that it can appear static. People wear almost the same expressions as those chipping at the Wall. It requires austere determination to stand in a queue made up of thousands. It cannot be a process familiar even to the most queue-hardened of these men and women; yet there seems to have been a kind of inner preparation for it, as if they've rehearsed the long, cold wait before, many times. And so the actual performance also partakes of a repeat, a rite.

No eyes are innocent, thinks the traveller. I cannot see the Brandenburger Tor as it is, as I would have seen it a year ago. This year – so strangely and effectively full of anniversaries – is its bicentenary. He supposes he would always have found it impressive, standing as it does at the end of the long Straße des 17 Juni that marches through the woods of the

Tiergarten, and heralding Unter den Linden ('the most beautiful street in the world' he hears his father's voice, sentimental-sob-choked, saying to him). But it could hardly be less to his taste, in its Graeco-Roman grandeur, with its six haughty columns, the Victory Quadriga surmounting it, terrible chariot and martial horses galloping eastwards. But now at last it *has* a heroic quality; anything less triumphant would not have done. The East–West *rapprochement* would be less imagination-haunting without this frankly *un*imaginative Neo-Classical monument, which suggests neither democracy nor peace, and yet – despite this, or indeed *because* of this – urges on those who believe passionately, and self-sacrificingly, in both.

He makes an inquiry of one of the guards at the pedestrians' gateway into East Berlin. The young guard, wearing an astrakhan hat and olive-coloured uniform, is all friendliness and smiles. No problem about going into East Berlin at all, he says, but *this* entrance is for Germans only (whether from West or East). *You*'ve still got to go in via either Checkpoint Charlie (he points in one direction) or Friedrichstraße (he gestures in the other). Neither will take long to get to.

The Reichstag, looming up on the far side of the gate, shows its porticoed, dark form against a gloomy sky. The traveller decides to go back the way he has come, as far as the Potsdamer Platz perhaps, and from there he'll make his way to the National Gallery. For more years than he can precisely estimate the Expressionists have addressed some of his profoundest apprehensions and longings. It'll be good to receive the visions of Kirchner and Nolde, Macke and Pechstein again.

'And may I wish you a happy Christmas,' says the East German guard.

HEILIG VATERLAND/DEUTSCHLAND (Holy Fatherland/Germany). Do these words, glowing out at him from the Wall, move him because they're ones he wasn't supposed to hear when younger? A candle concealed yet burning all this time. What did the painters of this slogan think of as 'holy'? Some Platonic Germany which absorbed, and then realised, the people's purest dreams, its noblest aspirations? Or the German *land*, particularly the forest that spreads over such a considerable area of both Germanies (all Germany), and in which as a small boy he had his own first intimations of the numinous?

If you can hear the Wall as well as see it, your hearing is also conditioned by your seeing. When the traveller turns his back to the Wall, looking out towards the naked trees of the Tiergarten, it sounds quite different. Now the tap-tappings, the chip-chippings are all but deafening. If I hadn't seen, and therefore didn't know, their origin, their perpetrators – thinks the traveller – I'd suppose myself to be listening to the activities of some hitherto undiscovered species. An addition to the world's fauna.

Later he learns that German – with its endless capacity for fresh compound words – has, these last weeks, evolved the term *Mauerspecht*, 'Wall-woodpecker' (better translated simply as Wallpecker). A person may arrive down the walks of the Tiergarten as an ordinary enough specimen of humankind, and find him/herself changed in minutes into a member of a new order brought about by these times.

And once a *Mauerspecht*, always one?

Strange that one can talk about 'these times' and specifically date their beginning, 9 November 1989, and everyone you address will have made the same reckoning, have the same awareness of having passed into a historical entity.

Thus to watch, or listen to, the *Mauerspechte* is to marvel anew at the profusion of Life, at its capacity for development, the same marvelling that the Expressionists knew as they submitted their senses and souls to Nature, and found without correspondences to what burned within.

For Emil Nolde (1867–1956) the calls of animals and birds came as colours. Consequently in his work colours also sing, call, shout . . . Surely in no other art-form is the interrelationship (one nearly says 'interchangeability') of the senses, and therefore of the medium, so powerfully suggested as in the true Expressionist painting. 'Everywhere,' said Emil Nolde, writing of a Baltic island where he went after his time in Berlin, 'my creatures stirred and lived their still or wild, lively lives, arousing my excitement and crying out to be painted . . .'*

Walking round the Nationalgalerie – the last completed

*See *The Expressionists* by Wolf-Dieter Dube, 1972.

work of Mies van der Rohe, severe yet also, in its imaginative functionalism, a place that emphasises, proclaims the basic equality of humans – the traveller is taken back to the hours, days, he has spent in the presence of German art, above all in Munich, a city with personal connections (in the late 1950s and 60s his father had held a directorship in a large chemical company there). The Lenbachhaus, the Neue Pinakothek, the Staatsgalerie Moderner Kunst, these had more than compelled him, they'd held him captive. His personal favourites – for there are always certain artists to whom, as Holden Caulfield says in *The Catcher in the Rye*, you want to write an intimate letter of thanks – soon became Franz Marc (1880–1916) and August Macke (1887–1914). They were close friends, both possessed of an extraordinary capacity for a joy that never ignores the atavistic, the elemental. Marc wrote:

Nature is everywhere, in us and outside us; but there is something which is not quite nature but rather the mastery and interpretation of nature: art. In its essence, art has always been the boldest removal from 'nature' and naturalness. The bridge across to the realm of the spirit, the necromancy of humanity.

Here was the wonderful paradox that Marc and his fellows embodied in their paintings: intensity of response to the natural, sensate world makes for different obligations than that of verisimilitude. First in importance is the capturing of the vital inner essence of living beings. The work of art, by virtue of its own organic life, can thus set up new relationships between the looker and the world outside the picture.

Marc's deer and woods, Macke's streets (like orchards of blossoms or fruit) have become permanent icons for the traveller. Were they what first made him realise that the Germany he knew as a child bequeathed him other things than images of a war-battered society, that part of his inability to settle down might be due to his being of German descent – with a German surname – and therefore heir to very different (and unconsciously held and transmitted) traditions than those of England?

In the Nationalgalerie Ernst Ludwig Kirchner (1880–1938) is as well represented as any of the other Expressionists, an artist who moved to Berlin in 1911 to capture the life of the city – more, the forces that animated the life in that city – in canvases that make people and houses all harmonise in one freed, spontaneous-seeming blend of colour that is song. People, attenuated, bend towards or in counterpart to each other, like some tracked-down animal species, in avenues, squares, bustling streets, that could be created not by man but by purely natural forces.

And standing before these works the traveller feels, as one can do almost every minute in Berlin, the grimness of the march the twentieth century has dragged this city on. Kirchner's Berlin is there no longer: the hubs he delighted in are precisely those areas now barren, the division between the Allied sectors and the East, into which the Wall was driven, and in which the *Mauerspechte* are now busy. *Those* at least Kirchner would have understood, rejoiced in; he'd have related them to the circus-folk whom he saw as dedicated to the release of appetites and talents stifled by conventional life.

Macke was killed in 1914, a month and a half after he'd been called up for military service. Marc perished in the carnage of Verdun in 1916. Kirchner was moved by the moral degeneracy of Nazi Germany – which had officially branded *him* as degenerate – to kill himself, in 1938.

Here is a painting which for years has fascinated the traveller, a work that connects the great Romantic spiritual works of Caspar David Friedrich with these Expressionists: Arnold Böcklin's *Die Toteninsel, The Island of the Dead*. In fact he has seen the place that inspired Böcklin's mystical work – a little island in the great gulf of Kotor, in southern Yugoslavia, and the time of seeing it imposes itself upon this present moment of reconfrontation.

Towards the cypresses, the walled church, and all the arcana of the islet a boat moves. How? Reverently? Fearfully? Proudly? That's the kind of place the *Hexe* and the *Gespenst* of that *Kasperltheater* of mine would have inspired, thinks the traveller, surprising himself by this vocabulary. And yet the boat belongs, like the painter himself, to that king I used to think of as God. All of us, all the time, are making a journey to some *Toteninsel*, and not just because we're going to die, because all those we know will die: always at every point there's waiting for us waste, deathliness, the realms of fear and sterility; we have to be mindful how we venture to them, how we steer the boat, how we effect a return journey (for that surely is an obligation).

'Panic and emptiness' – wasn't that what E. M. Forster saw as the antithesis of the golden triumphs Beethoven's

Fifth Symphony spoke of in its most confident bars? *Howard's End* has always been dear to the traveller because of its presentation of German-English relations.

And in it the half-German heroine speaks, he now recalls, of Böcklin:

> The German is always on the look-out for beauty. He may miss it through stupidity, or misinterpret it, but he is always asking beauty to enter his life, and I believe that in the end it will come. At Heidelberg I met a fat veterinary surgeon whose voice broke with sobs as he repeated some mawkish poetry. So easy for me to laugh – I, who never repeat poetry, good or bad, and cannot remember one fragment of verse to thrill myself with. My blood boils – well, I'm half German, so put it down to patriotism – when I listen to the tasteful contempt of the average islander for things Teutonic, whether they're Böcklin or my veterinary surgeon. 'Oh, Böcklin,' they say, 'he strains after beauty, he peoples Nature with gods too consciously.' Of course Böcklin strains, because he wants something – beauty and all the intangible gifts that are floating about the world . . .

In the enthusiasm of precocious adolescence he marked the passage, he recollects. Some of it sounds rather patronising now, even though the opposite effect was intended. (The English just don't seem to be able to keep their sense of superiority at bay, he says to himself.) But nevertheless there's truth in it, even in the eighty-year-old comparison between England and Germany. (And why *have* I turned out so rootless, so given to melancholy, the traveller reflects, why *are* means of transport and frontier-posts like homes to me?) There is, palpable even in the busy, confused Berlin of now, a straining, to use Forster's word, utterly absent from London.

'. . . In the end it will come', that entry of beauty. It didn't come during that orgy of nationalism and bloodshed that was the First World War, it was headed off in the last years of Weimar, perverted and then thrashed into nullity during the Third Reich, with its obscene parodies of the beautiful: the naphtha-lit parades, the revived *völkisch* ceremonials, the flashing of arms and the swooning cheerings-on by the crowds of girls. The Stalinist fervour of Ulbricht's East Germany cannot have gratified much craving for beauty. And the achievements of the Bundesrepublik, the 'Miracle' society, that had transformed a land of ruins and rubble, that of the traveller's earliest years, into one gleaming with chromium and glass, Western Europe's most economically powerful country . . . ?

Is Berlin beautiful? Can Böcklin's longing for beauty be said to have been met here?

What is it he finds, when leaving the house in which he's staying, walks down the prosperous, refined Fasanenstraße and enters the long, bright capitalist striding-forth of the Kurfürstendamm (the Ku'damm), into the shoppers' banquet of the Tauenzienstraße, culminating in the great store Ka De We (Kaufhaus des Westens: the Emporium of the West) and the bustle of the Wittenbergplatz? Isn't it a *kind* of beauty, though it's hard to imagine that being a prime desideratum of those who brought it all into being. At night when the lights blaze, and the wide streets are packed with cheerful people, still shopping – or pausing by one of the many booths that sell hot *Glühwein*, sweet biscuits cut into intriguing shapes, and all manner of toys and knick-knacks, while sending out synthetic German carols and folk-songs into the crowd – yes, downtown West Berlin *does* have beauty. It comes from being exactly what both citizens and a hetero-geneous assortment of others want it to be. Who'd quarrel with that as a definition? Certainly not the East Berliners who queue for their *Begrüßungsgeld* (welcome money), and want to spend it at shops and shows . . .

This beauty wouldn't be recognised as such by the city-planners of the Enlightenment, who created the boulevards and circuses that Occupation and Cold War have made into forlorn and unloved places through which the Wall still cuts. And it wouldn't be recognised by the great Prussians of the nineteenth century who saw their city become the capital of the Wilhelmine empire, with sombrely grand buildings – such as the Reichstag itself – to express the loftiness of its view of itself and its aims for the future. Those men and women of the Bauhaus, who wanted everything – even a chess-set – to be egalitarian, might have shuddered at so much opulence, so many temptations to spend, to have more. And though they must have seen it, the Ku'damm *et al.* cannot have been very dear to the architects who entered for the competition to make new-style homes in central Berlin – the Hansaviertel, where houses and apartment blocks, all light-honouring and with graceful, gentle lines, stand in urban woodland at the back of the Zoological Gardens.

But for the ordinary German, the ordinary Berliner. . .? Has this city, for forty years exactly a symbol of division, produced casts of mind that can be legitimately called 'ordi-nary'?

Or maybe it's the other way round: the tensions have made Germans, and Berliners in particular, more ordinary – in the sense of being more widely representative – than other Europeans. Who can retreat into *their* versions of ordinariness to escape the pressures of the here and now.

Whether the Wall is being manned by lethally armed guards or whether it's being chipped at by hosts of *Mauer-spechte*, it has effectively prevented Berliners from being escapists. Even when they *seek* escape – as in the multifarious night-life of the city – it is in the realisation of the deepest psychic urges and wishes. And this constant nag of demand-ing reality gives Berlin beauty too – even the Kreuzberg, even the abandoned-seeming townscape round the Askanischer Platz and Checkpoint Charlie, even now in the unions of bleak modern blocks and grandiose Prussian edifices that you encounter in East Berlin.

For Berlin, a city which never seems to rest or sleep, is the one real home of post-war European Man. And thinking this, the traveller – who for a long time now has been suffering from the depression that comes from his kind of homeless-ness – feels a very slight lifting-up of the heart.


Thoughts of home in a more literal sense come to him as he nears the house where he's staying with his friends. It's evening; in the lit windows of the apartments little Christmas trees show coloured lights. (As bigger ones did throughout the journey from the West–East German border into Berlin:

the endless-seeming fir forest would break to disclose clusters of small, steep-roofed, white-walled houses strangely similar to the toy ones he played with when young, and in the gardens of so many of these stood decorated *Tannenbäume!*)

There's something about the set of windows in German houses, something about the roofing of even quite tall apartment blocks, something too in the layout, the intersection of German streets – the traveller could draw it all, even with his eyes shut, but not explain it technically. Whatever it is it sends him back to years he'd once hoped entirely to bury, which have begun increasingly to haunt him, to ask questions of him, which may in all their sadness conceal matter to challenge this pervasive *present* sadness of his.

Which, as he enters the warmth of the Wilmersdorf house to have a drink with his friends, can, of course, be mitigated.

But just why has he come to Berlin?


On one level the question is easy to answer, in these days of smiling, welcoming border-guards and *Mauerspechte*: last month Berlin was transformed beyond optimists' dreams, and is still in a state of incredulous transformation.

Voices from the long queues before the barrier at Liverpool Street Station last week, everyone cold and impatient, yet quickened also by the wait for the train that would take them to Harwich and launch them towards this city:

'I felt I just had to go to Berlin for Christmas. I mean, I hadn't been intending to, at all. But I couldn't *not* go, after I'd seen all those wonderful pictures of the Wall being dismantled.'

'Well, *I* lived in Berlin for many, many years. *Loved* the place. It's true about its being a sort of island – well, Berliners call themselves *Insulaner*, you know, but what an island! I've got friends in both East and West. I'd give almost anything to go back in time and be there *in person* on 9 November itself. But the next best thing is to share Christmas and New Year with them all, isn't it?'

'The first time they can *really* be celebrated for fifty-seven years. Fifty-seven years!'

'Yes, they've been through a lot. They deserve all they're having now. They're saying the Brandenburg Gate will be open by Christmas Eve.'

(In fact it was opened before that, on the afternoon of Friday 22, in the presence of Helmut Kohl and Hans Modrow.)

And now inside this warm, well-appointed flat his own friends' voices, familiar, serious:

'What's so extraordinary is how 1989 has turned out to be such a replay of 1949, in reverse, I mean.'

(And for me, thinks the traveller – 1949 a return to England, 1989 a Christmas back in Germany. Even as he says this to himself, he feels a twitch on the curtains of the years that are his life, as if they are to go up and show him some truth about himself, about things, that he hasn't yet perceived.)

'I mean, think about 1949. The direct contrasts it makes with now are extraordinary.'

'Almost as if it was a coast with bays and promontories that fit the coast of *this* year.'

In January Stalin said Russia needed to tighten its grip on

Eastern Europe. On 1 February Hungary officially became a people's republic, and the very next day, the leader of the opposition fled to Vienna. Then another two weeks and the farce of the show-trial of Cardinal Mindszenty. In March the US ambassador to Poland said she was a Russian satellite. Poland demanded that the ambassador was recalled. But he was surely proved right when Poland annulled her friendship with Yugoslavia after Tito's break with Moscow. Hungary, Romania, Bulgaria and Czechoslovakia annulled theirs too very promptly.

There was constant harassment all that year of the Church, Catholic, Protestant and Orthodox, in Eastern Europe. In the Soviet Union Andrei Vishensky became the Foreign Minister, next in power as far as the rest of the world was concerned to Stalin himself. In September the West learned that the Soviet Union, seeking to rival the US, exploded an A-bomb in Kazakhstan. And it became the first country formally to recognise the People's Republic of China when the civil war finally ended and Mao Tse Tung was able to proclaim a Communist state from the Gate of Heavenly Peace.

And Germany?

'I myself know that the Berlin blockade and the airlift went on until May,' says the traveller.

'And what have we been hearing recently but cries of *Einheit! Einheit!*? In 1949 they were speaking of a unified Germany too. Remember what it meant then? The Russian ideal of a single, disarmed, neutered –'

'Neutered?'

'Neutral, and therefore neutered, Germany from whom reparations should be exacted. That was unacceptable. So –'

'Yes, I know,' says the traveller, his father's face suddenly exceedingly clear before him, 'on 23 May 1949 the Bundesrepublik Deutschland was declared.'

'The DDR on 7 October.'

'And Berlin became the anomalous place it's been ever since, a wedge driven through it – even twelve years before the Wall – thus sundering one of the greatest cities of the world. The West is a legal island, surrounded by another country of which the city's eastern and lesser half is the capital. West Berlin is not allowed to be a capital, is not even part of West Germany: official documents have to be signed on behalf of West Germany *and* the western part of Berlin. It isn't subject to the West German Parliament, though that in effect controls it. And it is still occupied territory. There's still a British sector, a French sector and an American one. The Zones live on . . .'

'And with them, then, just a bit of 1949,' says the traveller.

He is almost comforted by this; so much mental reorganisation is needed as 1989 moves to its close. He suddenly sees in his mind's eye that map of Europe he'd first gazed on, so neat and clear-seeming, in Roderick Meiklejohn's School Atlas. How could an atlas of today show you the Europe of *now* – the melting of the divide in Berlin, the chaos in Timisoara and Bucharest, from which all are now tensely awaiting news . . .

He drops cubes of ice in his glass of whisky. Tonight he will not sleep too badly; Berlin, excited, hyperactive indeed, has given him rest where London didn't. With thoughts of not just a year ending but a decade, and of all that hasn't happened, and of all that he has failed to achieve, to realise, he has lain awake sometimes for the entirety of a night. Under the great feather counterpane of a German bed, such as had taken care of his sleep forty years back, things have been better . . .

He's travelling on the Berlin U-Bahn, on one of its trains which glide through the underground tunnels, with a pleasant voice announcing each station before it stops. The seats are red, the walls wood-lined, the floor clean – all so different from the filthy Tube of London . . . *'Nächste Station,'* says the cultured female voice, *'Essen, Bredeney.'* But Essen doesn't *have* a Metro system, the traveller thinks. Or does it *now*? He can't remember. For he *has* been back there since his childhood, to a town not just whole, but gleaming with success. Nevertheless he gets out, and walks along the platform to the escalator. He's curious as to what he'll find when he reaches the top and the cold night air.

Wind slaps him in the face; it's very dark. German towns are so well lit as a rule. He looks round him. Though he does not recognise *where* he is, *when* is not hard to answer. Some point between 1945 and 1949. In the square in which he's arrived the great shells of buildings loom up; behind them and beside them are the stinking piles of rubble he once knew so well. Somewhere the people must be hiding. Are Matthias and his wife and their little son, Klaus, here? Is it behind one of these gaunt uncertain walls that their home was?

Music accosts him, borne on the wind. He knows what it is before he catches consecutive bars:

*Stille Nacht, heilige Nacht!*
*Alles schläft, einsam wacht*
*nur das traute hochheilige Paar.*
*Holder Knabe im lockigen Haar,*
*schlaf in himmlischer Ruh,*
*schlaf in himmlischer Ruh . . .*

How odd of him; he didn't notice it when he got out at the exit to the U-Bahn. In the middle of this *Platz* there's a Christmas tree, taller than those in the Wilmersdorf windows, taller than those in the East German gardens the express train had pulled him past – more like those at either side of the Brandenburger Tor. It will take a lot of decorating; its branches are devoid of adornment now, they look like dark-green, spiky-feathered wings.

And just as he's thinking this, they come along, his parents. Bedecking the Christmas tree was one of the very few domestic tasks his father gave any sign of enjoying.

The traveller realises now, of course, that it's all nonsense, that his mother and father are dead. As in many a previous dream (and he has no doubt that this *is* a dream, though there's little he can do about the fact) their funerals are swiftly shown – in a few seconds of demonstration by them – to have been mistakes, stupidly interpreted, not least by himself. Really he's quite pleased to see them. This'll be the first Christmas they've been all together since . . . The tree, he notices, is soughing and bending in the wind, which, while he's been listening to the proofs against the funerals, has been growing in strength. Its trunk sways violently, first to one side then to another. Perhaps it'll break!

'What's going to happen here?' his mother asks him.

'*Something* must happen here,' says his father, 'mustn't it?'

They swing towards him so that, near-blinded by the furious wind though he is, he can see their faces properly, and, of course, they're more those of dead people than of living ones. Their bones protrude through the dark, discoloured flesh:

> *nur das traute, hochheilige Paar.*
> *Holder Knabe im lockigen Haar. . .*

But he's not a curly-haired little boy any more, for his mother to kiss and his father to point things out to on Roderick Meiklejohn's atlas; he's a middle-aged man, he's a traveller.

A voice says through the city square – or is it through the bedroom?

> *. . . der Tod ist ein Meister aus Deutschland*

(Death is a master from Germany)

He's awake now, though for a minute he doesn't know where, maybe stranded, boatless, on that *Toteninsel*. How stupid, even in a dream, to have thought that his parents weren't dead. His mother died almost exactly twenty-four years ago, his father seventeen. A few weeks before her death his mother said: 'I've really very little happiness to look back on.' And his father, as he lay ill, declared: 'I *had* a good mind, but what have I done with it?'

We have always built walls. We have built them to protect ourselves. They have been built around people, around political systems and around religious beliefs.

They have even been built around human concerns; around Eros, love and partnership.

*der Tod ist ein Meister aus Deutschland*

Is he himself afraid of death? He hardly knows any more. He used to be, before his parents died. He raises himself up in bed; through the venetian blinds he can see the lights in other apartments across the courtyard. In his head so much is jumbled up, the years, the personal and the political, the English and the German, experiences and fantasies.

> *Schwarze Milch der Frühe wir trinken dich nachts*
> *wir trinken dich mittags der Tod ist ein Meister aus Deutsch-*
>   *land*
> *wir trinken dich abends und morgens wir trinken und trinken*
> *der Tod ist ein Meister aus Deutschland sein Auge ist blau*
> *er trifft dich mit bleierner Kugel er trifft dich genau . . .*

(Black milk of daybreak we drink you at night/we drink you at noon death is a master from Germany/we drink you at sundown and in the morning we drink and drink you/death is a master from Germany his eyes are blue/he strikes you with leaden bullets his aim is true . . .)* Death is what those German cities of his childhood had secretly taught him. Death was the master of the year in which he was born. For there are ages when much dying is done, and he'd arrived in the world during one of them.

*Paul Celan: 'Todesfuge' ('Death Fugue') from *Poems of Paul Celan*, trans. Michael Hamburger (1989).

Before turning in for the night he and his friends here had been speaking of the Cold War, now suddenly over, to cheers and embraces and tears from all peoples. But they could have spoken of the real war that had brought the cold one about, have recited another litany:

> One Dutchman in eleven
> One German in ten
> One Yugoslav in nine
> One Russian in eight
> One Pole in six
> One Jew in two
> Dead!

Half a million German civilians killed during the saturation bombing of the country! Their deaths had cried out to him through the spaces of Essen, Dortmund, Hamburg . . .

He should have known that Christmas-time in Germany, however great the jubilation around him, however brightly the future shone, would bring back to him past sorrows – which were still present ones in millions of minds.

Learning the facts behind his (child's) suspicions had been very painful. He now carries these facts around with him everywhere, like data of his person and life. Essen first received a British bomb, a new four-thousand-pound one, aimed at Krupp's, on the night of Sunday, 22 March 1942. Four days later the entire Ruhrgebiet was heavily bombarded by two hundred RAF planes. On the night of 30 May Cologne received over two thousand tons of bombs; hundreds of acres of the city were devastated. In March 1943 the Battle of the Ruhr took place, which saw the flattening of four hundred

133

acres of Düsseldorf, and the dropping of a further thousand tons of bombs on Essen itself. Just over two months later the RAF swooped down on the two great Ruhr dams, the Eder and the Mohne. Ursula – who'd looked after the traveller's baby brother – may have survived, but almost two thousand people did not. Mülheim and Dortmund, already heavily punished from the air, were now deluged into inoperability and lifelessness; the waters entered mines and underground shelters. Nor did the raids end there; the last six months of the war saw the intensification of aerial attacks.

While Essen was indisputably a centre of heavy industry producing arms (and indeed continued to be so right until the end of the war), Cologne, following the example of Lübeck, was chosen as a target not for strategic reasons but because it was large and psychologically significant. (Lübeck had been selected because it was 'easier than most cities to destroy'.) Air Marshal Sir Arthur Harris urged that 'the claims of smaller towns' should not be neglected, a strange expression since it suggests towns, of no industrial or military importance, begging not to be left out. And they weren't.

What usually took place at the beginning of the 'terror-bombing' was this: the planes came over at night (what cosmic blasphemy there is in the term 'bomber's moon'!) and grouped themselves above a town. Certain planes would then drop bombs to start fires; the other planes would then unload their cargo on to these fires to augment them. In certain weather conditions fire-storms would start, maelstroms of flames which the winds widened and widened. The rate of devastation and death could thus be very rapid, and was to become even more so as the war spurred on

British technical progress and involved the Americans. Fifty thousand died in Hamburg on one night, forty thousand on another; in Pforzheim seventy thousand people died in twenty minutes, and an American commentator travelling with a film crew was able to announce to his nation: 'A city is being wiped out before your eyes. Nothing can live in this inferno!'

And Berlin – the city whose beauty the traveller has been debating? In January 1943 it was hit by the first ever daylight raids. In November 1943 'Bomber' Harris declared that it would be bombed until 'the heart of Nazi Germany ceases to beat'. Even by then its beating must have been irregular, impaired. It was 'pounded' (that favourite word of the times) yet again that month, and again the next, and in January 1944 the largest bomb-tonnage to be unloaded so far was dropped on it. So by 20 January something like thirty thousand tons had made the name 'Berlin' refer to a place utterly unlike what its syllables had previously conjured up.

Certainly 1949 stands behind 1989. But so does 1939 – another significant anniversary in this year of anniversaries and reversals.

In this city of gladness many other people too must be being kept awake by memories prompted by the occasion, date speaking to date. As if one were bound on a permanent wheel of remembering. And perhaps one is.

Sinking his head into the pillows, the traveller conjures up the German young of his 1940s life: Hannelore, Günter, deep into middle age now, and probably parents (and possibly grandparents) themselves. How clearly they stand before him, Hannelore with her plaits and her mouth open in song,

Günter with his patched trousers and his harmonica. And then there's Achim . . .

But it's a curious, and as yet inexplicable thing, that whereas he can see all the other people from Essen very vividly, the image of Achim eludes him utterly. His mother later pointed out to him boys who (apparently) resembled him, so he has an idea of his appearance, but of Achim himself he can recall nothing – not a word, not a gesture, not a look. And yet for months he lived in the room adjoining his own one.

Christmas in its showing-forth of the new-born baby is the showing-forth of the innocence within man. The adoration of the infant Christ is the respect we give to that innocence, albeit often very grudgingly or covertly. The animals kneeling down in the stable demonstrate in *Krippe* after *Krippe* the love that exists deep down between us and the creature-world, yet also reflect our guilt, as if we are needing (as surely we are) some gesture from it that shows we are forgiven for our outrages upon it. Though officially the Christian churches proclaim belief in original sin (not in fact included in Christian dogma until the fourth century), the icons of its most popular festival enunciate quite the opposite interpretation of the world. Man *au fond* – in his naked, newly arrived condition – is good, and can bring out goodness all over the created world, from stars which shine the more brightly to oxen and donkeys which he wants to include in his happiness.

The traveller goes into East Berlin for Christmas Eve. Innocence has truly descended on the guards and officials. Never has he been wished pleasant days and compliments of the season so extensively and smilingly as on 24 December 1989 at Friedrichstraße Station, East Berlin.

He remembers that very first visit of his to East Germany twenty-two years before . . .


Very early in the morning of a summer's day, when there is only a flush of dawn-light in the sky, the great express comes to a stop in the middle of forestland. Everything is very quiet, inside and outside the train.

This quiet, however, is broken by an unmistakable sound, that of machine-gun fire, volleys of it somewhere in the mist-filled forest. People pretend not to be nervous, self-consciously get out breakfast stuff or pick up books. Then the train moves on, only to halt just beyond a look-out post by which is a large notice announcing:

DIE DEUTSCHE DEMOKRATISCHE REPUBLIK
DER ANTINAZISTAAT


And now the wait is so long that further forward motion becomes almost unimaginable. Guards appear, in round helmets, long trench coats and high boots. Inspection of passports, visas, tickets, takes an immense time, and it's absurd to feign insouciance. Though you can be tolerated in transit, on German Democratic territory you are an intruder.

And throughout all the journeys through the country this feeling is endorsed. At the bigger stations rifle- or bayonet-holding soldiers are positioned on high places, vigilant, it seems, for any possibly subversive behaviour. When the train draws up alongside a platform, soldiers step forward grimly to prevent any passenger tempted to descend. They wear their faces as they do their helmets.

At this very Friedrichstraße Station, two decades ago, the traveller stood in a queue kept in control by armed men. In it you weren't supposed to talk to one another; the traveller said something to his friend, and immediately a guard came towards him, weapon at the alert, and rebuked him. His friend protested; he was ordered out of the line, like a small child. When they finally were able to enter East Berlin, it was with feelings of exhaustion and tension. These were not relieved by an unexpected encounter with soldiers goose-stepping down the street towards one of the official buildings over which they stood guard. Jackboots banged hard upon the tarmac, and the faces beneath the helmets seemed quite dehumanised.

And less than a week ago, the goose-step was abolished. 'Enjoy yourself in East Berlin,' says the young official who lets the traveller in.


Through the Brandenburger Tor, past the Christmas tree and up Unter den Linden they come, the West Germans, ceaselessly it seems. Unter den Linden, that his father had so loved!

It's rather dreary now; the countless visitors do not really enliven it. And looking eastwards as the avenue, changing into the Karl-Liebknecht-Straße, marches towards the Alex-

138

anderplatz, the prospect is equally bleak. Prussia stands continually islanded (often literally by gracefully bridged canals) against the ocean of cheerless materialism triumphant, a looking-glass version of the Miracle Germany, all façade, all modernity. And yet . . . it is *this* Berlin that has proved itself brave, strong-willed, seething with hope these last weeks. These qualities cannot have sprung from nowhere; people have in the end always been superior to the edifices that attempt to define them.

Periodically, through these rather empty streets, with mostly smelly Trabants driving down them, the smart cars of West Germans roar past, capitalism saluting aspiring capitalism. But the demeanour of East Germans has a rather beguiling ingenuousness about it, a child's pleasure that things are going right, and this somehow renders very brash the more strident visitors and enhances the world-weariness that too many from Western Europe, like the traveller himself perhaps, tend to impart.

Yet Christmas itself – well, *this* Christmas – like some Dickensian Spirit has affected them all.

The porch of the Dom contains notices about a series of seminars on homosexuality, discussions on all aspects of the subject, psychological, sociological, political, religious. There are posters pleading for support to be given to Romania now fighting so bloodily for its freedom. (These, in fact, have been visible all over the city; news has come today of the capture of the Ceauşescus and the affirmation of the National Salvation Committee.) Inside the Dom it's Northern Baroque gone musty and mouldy, patches of damp disfiguring the eggshell walls, the gilt on all the decorative motifs tarnished.

The choir is up in the balcony, eager to begin, but still the congregation – which the traveller joins – grows. In they come from the cold, twilit boulevard, many of them vigorously, almost ostentatiously young – fleece-lined anoraks above those stone-bleached jeans. To be in church, particularly on a major feast-day, shows us – their movements say, their very way of taking seats – to be serious, energetic and ready to defy. It's not hard to imagine these boys and girls crying out *Einheit!*, waving the German national flag, breaking into the offices of the Stasi and throwing files out of windows in protest.

But the pastor himself brings back earlier times, not those of Ulbricht and Honecker, still less those of Hitler's Reich, but those of a Prussia, even before unification, the quiet Protestant solemnity that you encounter in the characters of Theodor Fontane. He reminds the congregation (as if they needed it!) of the very special nature of this Christmas, when Germans, Berliners of both East and West, have been able to draw together in friendship, to realise how contrary to God is division of His people. And surely they're drawing together too to worship Him (the traveller sees in his mind that gold-crowned being from the *Kasperltheater*, the king whose cloak could cover the world), whose only wish is that we should all love each other.

Tears run down the red face of the plump man on the traveller's right; by his clothes, that rather dashing leather jacket, he judges him to have come from the West.

'And we pray too for those in Romania, whose sufferings shock us all – so many brutally killed, so many wounded.

Our hearts go out to them in their hour of need, and our hopes for their victory over un-Christian tyranny.'

(Only weeks ago East Germany's officialdom was trying to smuggle sensitive documents into Romania; the Ceauşescu regime was the one uncorrupted ally of Honecker's socialist state. And having discomfited himself with this thought – for it disturbs the serene picture he wants of a reformed East Germany gliding as smoothly as one of the new U-Bahn trains towards the West – then the traveller entertains another one. The men who made up the first East German government had put themselves through dangers worthy to rank with those the Christian martyrs exposed themselves to. Imprisonment, torture. At the beginning of the country's life it determined to do all it could to create a non-Nazi, more, an anti-Nazi clerisy, pushing through programmes of educating teachers to guide the young in just and egalitarian ways. Why, the traveller wonders, must I be made to think of all these many diverse people as contributors only to repression?)

The singing has begun now. His father and mother had been right – the traveller, who has journeyed much, thinks – no people can sing as sweetly as Germans. And no language sounds as beautiful, whether in a Bach chorale or in one of Schönberg's songs defying conventional tonality . . .


> *O du fröhliche, o du selige,*
> *gnadenbringende Weihnachtszeit!*


(Oh, you joyful, oh, you blessed, mercy-bringing Christmas-time!) It was absurd for tears to be welling in *his* eyes too. It must be the example of those around him, for many of the congregation are crying now. Perhaps it's the full-to-overflowing condition of the interior, perhaps it's the thought of all that's happened in the world outside the church walls, that's moving everybody. And personal memories also, of course. The traveller sees them all before him, by the grandfather clock in Tirpitzstraße 49, where they put the tree, Daddy, Mummy, Toni, Trude, Günter, Hannelore, all the rifts of international and of domestic war temporarily obliterated.

And now, inevitably, it's *'Stille Nacht, heilige Nacht!'*, the most Germanic melody in the world, fuller and more charged with longing even than in his dream. Had I seen tears in my father's eyes, the traveller says to himself, as indeed in these circumstances I undoubtedly would have done, I'd have muttered, 'Stupid German sentimentality.'

> *Alles schläft, einsam wacht*
> *nur das traute hochheilige Paar.*
> *Holder Knabe im lockigen Haar . . .*

I mustn't be lulled into comfortable deception, he chides himself. The song is quite ridiculous. How could anyone know (or care) that Christ, when a baby, had curly hair? It's not innocence you find in productions like this, it's exploitation of innocence, a casting of screens (walls, if you prefer) round the disagreeables of life.

And yet who could deny that the Berliners had truly known these?

*
**142**

Via the Brandenburger Tor they continue to come, on foot, into East Berlin, even in this ebbing of a cold day, even though they will find nothing that caters for or pleases a tourist, everything being emphatically shut. From his present perspective the great gate appears not the monumental divide it has for so long been, but rather what it was intended to be – the half-way point, solemnly marked, of a great parade down which a people confident in its identity can make its way. Even though *these* people have a deliberately casual air about them.

This has indeed been a year of the movement of Germans – first all those from the East who, in the summer, streamed determinedly over the Hungarian border into West Germany, and later over the Czech one. These heralded the immigrants who made the crossing, at last legitimate, over their own border, and those who are still making it; about three hundred thousand have already passed into West Germany to lead a new life there. In addition to this self-evacuation from the East, there is the constant to-ing and fro-ing of Germans from one part of Berlin to the other, one part of Germany to the other. Just as the *Mauerspechte* are a new species, so do these (differently) moving Germans establish themselves as new developments within their kind. They've not existed as such before. And they know this.

At this very moment, all over the world, conference-rooms, board-rooms, newspaper offices, bars, clubs, cafés, private homes buzz with talk of the reunification of Germany. Could it really happen? And if so, how? when? Some of the talk will be charged with a hope the speakers dare not quite articulate in public, some of it with a dread or a resentment that equally, outside a private context, will be edited through diffidence and diplomacy. In the traveller's own country Mrs Thatcher says that German reunification is not on the agenda at the moment; it's a possibility in ten to fifteen years' time. Here in East Germany Hans Modrow has also said it's not on the agenda; augmented relations between the two countries, yes, exchanges on business and on cultural levels, yes, but their becoming one, no! not to be thought of yet. Gorbachev too pronounces: not on the agenda. What a meaningless phrase this is, since agenda are given to politicians by events. *Wir sind ein Volk!* is the rallying-cry in Leipzig, Berlin, Dresden. The people are saying that it *is* on an agenda, because it's on *their* agenda.

These last weeks, thinks the traveller – who feels for the leader and government of his Britain a loathing he shares with almost everyone he knows, and who has felt battered and reduced by them – these last weeks may mark a turning-point in our regard for those in high places. Increasingly those places are being exposed as over-remote. Every week this past half-year has witnessed a bending of politicians seemingly convinced of their own judgement yet perforce acknowledging another – that of the *Volk*.

In both Berlins you can read Chancellor Kohl's statement: '*Die Einheit wird kommen, wenn die Menschen in Deutschland sie wollen.*' (Unity will come, if the people in Germany themselves want it.) And – even honouring the enormous part played in affairs by Gorbachev himself – who can doubt the steamrolling actuality of German wishes?

For, in a very real sense – thinks the traveller, threading his way towards Friedrichstraße Station through the still-incoming crowd, grey in the evening light – the reunification of Germany has already happened. Again and again German friends have told him that, after all these years, it's not really possible to tell, from his or her way of talking, an East from a West Berliner. When the Germans of both countries come together to sing carols – as this afternoon in the Dom – they share in the same imaginative, ideal world preserved in tradition, a world he himself was privileged to partake of at an early and formative stage of his life.

(Some, of course, would see it as more than that, as a victory for individualistic Christianity. Certainly no Christmas has ever seemed more *Christ*mas than this one – celebrated enthusiastically where for years it has been apologised for, and worse, and with the Supreme Soviet having pronounced officially the death of Marx's anti-God, having said that religion is not merely the opiate of a people after all, but corresponds to . . . well, to what? To deep needs or to truths? They are not after all the same thing.)


A large crowd of people, East Germans, West Germans, visitors to Berlin from a whole diversity of countries, are gathered at the barriers at Friedrichstraße Station. It's ridiculous and anachronistic to feel a mild tension at the presentation of passport and one-day visa, to feel a mild relief when it's obvious that you're back in West Berlin again. But mental habits take a long time to die. 'These days anything is possible,' he has been told repeatedly by Berliners, but possible too are reactions, gestures, immediate images coming from the recent past. The present takes a long time, requires indeed a large slice of the future, to become the dimension in which you easily live.

From the bends of the elevated S-Bahn vast areas of both Berlins present themselves, lit up now, so that they're rendered by both darkness and light extraordinarily alike. Between them the icy-looking waters of the Spree and the stark spaces where life had once been so busy and so delightful that Kirchner had celebrated it with canvases whose colours sang like tropical birds.

*'Ich bin ein Berliner'* – these words of John F. Kennedy must be the most famous spoken by any non-German about the post-war city, words that had (apparently) moved many real Berliners. The traveller has always felt that he would *not* have been of their number, since, no matter from what lofty or kindly motive it is made, a claim to another's identity will surely be an impertinence. He feels that it would be wrong to appropriate the very particular emotions about their city the dismantling of the Wall must have brought about in today's Berliners; *he* does not know the pain of having relations sealed off from one by political barriers, or the strange pleasure of being again in places you'd always thought of as extensions of yourself. Nevertheless it's true that, in a way, he *does* feel the divided city to be mirrored in his own psyche: the Western side standing for energy, liberalism, libertarianism, the Eastern for restraint, control, checks against the pleasure principle. And now the changed city with its demoted Wall, its *Mauer zu verkaufen*, must enter the recesses of one's being, and that will prove harder than

it appears in these days of the situation's newness: 'We have always built walls. We have built them to protect ourselves.'

Certainly the traveller would find it hard to say *Ich bin ein Berliner*; and yet, by dint of its anomalous confusions, Berlin could be a more appropriate spiritual home than any – of a people but not yet of a nation-state, reflecting the world but engrossed in a kaleidoscope-like shaking-up of its own constituent elements. Always the traveller has been fascinated by lines, walls, divisions inside a society that cause one set of people to be placed on one side, another on the opposing one. It began, he supposes, in the days of the Occupation of Germany, when the legal separation of British from Germans was something daily refuted by his intimate personal life. To such an extent that at times he could feel he belonged, had he to make the choice, to the opposite side of the dividing line to that in which officialdom (and accident of birth) had placed him. Since then many lines have exerted fascination for him: the Mason-Dixon Line in the United States and the line within that, between black and white; the lines of the Spanish Civil War, and the invisible lines that these bequeathed to the later Spain; the line increasingly imposed upon his own country, between supporters and beneficiaries of the Thatcher government and those like himself hostile to it. He has stood on the other side of the wall imposed on sexual relations by certain laws, both moral and civic; he has entered (is it the realm of the goats?) the territory of the non-believers that the believers see as opposed to theirs. (For, despite the muddle of his religious opinions and feelings, he is sure that he belongs, on any dogmatically formulated terms, to the non-believers.)

But though he had felt German in Occupation Germany, it was impossible to sever his links of blood and love with the British; if he detested the divides in America, he'd also been compelled by the separatist cultures these had produced; his time in Spain had made him able to sympathise with lives spent – out of devotion to the Catholic faith or to a particular region – on what he still will call 'the wrong side'. And in his own agnostic position, he knows many yearnings towards some definition of a God, many tendernesses for the personality of Christ.

And if at the moment he finds it hard to cross the line drawn in his own country, he knows that this is because the war to impose it is still going on (and therefore claiming his services). And because behind the Thatcherite attempt at hegemony lies the vast force of market materialism. And that's as ugly a wall as ever bestrode Berlin.

Back in the brilliance and activity of the Ku'damm as *Weihnachtsabend* accelerates traffic and people, he makes for the Kaiser Wilhelm Church, the gaunt 'Broken Tooth' that the city has preserved to remind visitors and citizens of the destruction once visited upon it, and now linked to the polygon of a new church with windows of iridescent blues. Making his way through the pedestrian passage between them the traveller comes across a line of people, of both sexes and all ages, standing with long flaming brands in their hands and with little candles at their feet. The hands that are not holding the torches are supporting placards. He pauses to read them, receiving at once from this still and serious group a sense of goodness and heartfelt concern for life.

DER GOTT DER MENSCHEN IST AUCH DER GOTT

DER TIERE

he reads. (The God of men is also the God of animals.) And again:

DENKEN SIE EINMAL DARAN, WIE DIE TIERE FÜR

UNSERE WEIHNACHTSBRÄUCHE LEIDEN MÜSSEN.

(Just think for once how animals must suffer for our Christmas customs.)

The traveller asks a woman in the centre (she has the air somehow of being the band's coordinator) if he may join them in their vigil. His request is granted. For here is acknowledgement of perhaps the final and most fiercely guarded wall of them all, that between man and animals. That must be dismantled too. The preposterous usurpations, denials of rights must be confronted, resisted, brought down – so that animals and men can stand together as joint occu- piers of this earth. The God that somewhere the traveller has always carried within him could no more countenance this rejection of beings He's made and watches over than He could the repudiation or enslavement by one group of humans of another.

He thinks of animals he's known and loved, of animals that have moved him simply by existing, that have humbled and yet inspired him by the sheer quiddity of their beings.

He thinks of how man, erecting complex structures of philosophy, empirical and metaphysical, to excuse himself, has dealt destruction to the animal world – for food, for fur, out of fear and, most evilly of all, for sport. All of a sudden, as he, in the silence of the watch, with a flared torch burning in his right hand, composes his thoughts on animal matters, he feels that the child of Tirpitzstraße would have joined this protest. He who had enjoyed such a tender friendship with Debs, who had felt emanations from that abandoned menagerie in the Bredeney woods, who knew even then what Awe at the natural world (*from* the natural world) meant, *he* would have said, seeing that placard, *'Ja, der Gott der Menschen ist auch der Gott der Tiere.'*

After an hour of silent demonstration the group breaks up. As the traveller is greeted and made welcome, he thinks: It's strange. It's being back in Germany, I suppose, and having a year and a decade coming to a close, and the beginning of another century now in sight – but I feel a desire to see that small boy again; there is so much surely that we should say to one another. And that's another line, another wall, the one between the remote past and the present. I've tended to guard myself against the child I was, and no doubt, in choosing to do so, I've been dictated to, like all wall-builders, principally by my fears.


Christmas morning has come again to the world; its saviour has been born with bells that ring out through the city and also within the traveller's head. Swinging one way they make a sadness resound through the chambers of his mind – so much suffering that he hasn't even attempted to relieve, so much that he hasn't done, made impotent perhaps by the power of the past. But swinging the other way they deliver him happiness – on behalf of others, for beyond doubt this is the happiest Christmas Berliners have known for the entire duration of his own life, and for many years before that. He remembers the voices from the Liverpool Street queue . . .

When it's the sadness that swings through him, he thinks of England, of what has made up too great a part of his life there. On that Dutch ferry he'd half known, hadn't he, that he'd find there the hardness, the snobberies, the perpetual fault-finding that he'd noted in the British community in Essen? That lack of confrontation with the terrible things they'd carried out, that inability to see that bombing was wicked, that occupation was unjust. He'd only have been foreseeing the truth if he had entertained such misgivings. Official England, the England of the schools and institutions with which he'd had to do, brought him repeated misery, which dominates his life even now. The private establishments to which he was sent – preparatory school and public school – were occupied territory, if you like, where only conformity could bring you any ease. The Army's officers had not only to be obeyed, but saluted. Of course he knew friendship, the pleasures of knowledge, stabs of the numinous, but they all came *despite* the system, not because of it. The friendships had been a bit like the 'fraternisings' that – irregularly – went on in the teeth of instructions during the British Occupation's first months. And the joys of his boyhood and adolescence resembled those flowering weeds that grew upon the ruins of the bombed cities – indomitable and

151

delightful Nature, that even man's determination to do as much damage as his demon could drive him to, was unable to vanquish.

His parents brought home to England from Germany a never-dying sense of personal defeat. His father never recovered from the death of Finette – from his guilt at having loved her, from his sorrow that their love knew no proper fulfilment. And he too was affected by the devastation of the Germany he'd so loved; he'd taken photograph after photograph of the damage. (The album that contained these served to keep vigorous the traveller's memory of the places of his early years.) He was disappointed by the meanness of British attitudes to Europe, attitudes that intensified with the years and the enforced change in Britain's world-role.

In his work his father pursued the ideals of European unity, was a keen supporter of British entry into the Common Market, and served on international committees for industrial development; he became the director of the German subsidiary of a large British chemical firm based in Munich. But his private life was soured by his inability to overcome the bitter wounds of the German years. He did not find adequate compensation in his family life, which indeed appeared to frustrate him more than anything else. He would often study his elder son with eyes of resentment, for it was he, not the younger boy, who'd witnessed the affair with Finette, the corrosion of his marriage, the beginning of his surrender to drink. He knew all this was not forgotten – nor forgiven. It did not make for a very happy relationship – and by the time the two of them realised that they had many interests and ideals in common, it was too late. His mother dead, the son drew closer to his father, on whom the effects of years of heavy drinking were beginning to be marked and dangerous. His last years were very terrible ones, of great mental and physical agony. When he was dying, he would talk to the traveller about his Europeanism: about his belief in European monetary union, for instance. It was like a bequest to the living, his only one, in fact, for he had mismanaged his affairs into virtual bankruptcy. The traveller received it with a certain ambivalence, because he – illogically – tended to hold his father's extreme Germanophilia responsible for the fatal difficulties of his unsatisfactory life . . .

*der Tod ist ein Meister aus Deutschland sein Auge ist blau*
*er trifft dich mit bleierner Kugel er trifft dich genau . . .*

Shortly before he died, the father received a letter from a publisher, accepting what he'd sent of a book on industrial management and the European community. His sadness that he would never complete it must have been subsumed by other sadnesses; he wrote to the traveller a letter saying how he wished he could have been a better father to the son he loved so much.

It was a few months after his death that the traveller came across a wallet in a box full of letters and personal documents. He opened the wallet to find a photograph of Finette, beautiful, distinct, and, in the pocket opposite this, a collection of letters tied up in frayed ribbon. To read them was an alarming experience, it made the pulse race, the saliva dry in the mouth. Of course he had never doubted that the long-dead woman and his father had had a relationship; some stupid inner reticence had made him unable to imagine the mutual passion they had known. Page after page made this passion at last eloquent to him, not shying away from intimate detail or from expression of hopes for its possible life-long duration.

Most of the other letters in the same box were from Fr Martindale, answering complex, almost scholastic questions on Catholic dogma, and expressing an understanding of the crisis he was facing within his marriage. The letters – containing theological particularities beyond the traveller's comprehension – cannot have been as effective as their writer must have wished. His father died without the consolations of any faith, faced death as his wife had done – as an agnostic – and as doubtless his son, the traveller, will do . . .

The traveller's mother found far greater self-fulfilment than did her husband in her relationship with her sons. She was unsparing of herself, fiercely, unfairly emotional in her dealings with them, compelling them to share – or at least partake of – her unpredictable changes from joy to melancholy, anger to acceptance, worldly ambition to a poetic apprehension of the visible world that she'd first known in her solitary country girlhood. At times her elder son thought she made life into an opera; he longed for the simple spoken lines of a straight play. It was only many years afterwards that he came to understand – partly through scrutiny of his own temperament – that his mother's apparent emotionalism was really a cover for a detachment, of which she was perhaps herself rather frightened. Behind or beyond the adoration and the outrage that she expressed so abundantly and equally was a profoundly moral objectivity, pitiless, ever vigilant, infinitely attentive. It made her not feel as warm as she would have liked to have felt, and she tried to disguise her coldness with outward professions of affection where, in fact, only a more or less kindly indifference existed. The traveller has done likewise.

She had detested the garrison society of Occupation Germany, its cultivated hedonism, its bored little adulteries, its languid superiority over the occupied. While by no means sympathetic to her husband's philo-Germanic enthusiasms, she later kept up – and indeed improved – her German, and the only social functions to which she ever accompanied him were those concerning Anglo-German relations. Though not very musical, she delighted in the German folk-songs that Toni and Trude had taught her and her son, and remembered them all.

But – thinks the traveller sadly – I have to reprimand them across the years, across the line that separates the living from the dead. His parents – they were alike in this – may have disliked the Occupation and its mores, but nevertheless they were part of it. Similarly, back in England, while they themselves may have been freer than many around them of certain presumptions and snobberies, they did not withdraw from the great occupation of the country that the upper and middle classes had established. They wanted parts in it, not so much for themselves as for their offspring. The consequences for those on the other side of the border of the system they supported never seemed much to preoccupy them.

For himself, ever since leaving Germany the traveller has never wanted to be part of an occupying force again. He's preferred to be among the occupied. He has desired all his life a society where such terminology isn't valid. At one time such a society had been envisaged as a Communist one; these last months full confrontation with the unreality of this vision has been inescapable. Not that the traveller ever thought it had been realised in Eastern Europe. A visitor there, from his early twenties onwards, he'd taken in the oppressions and resentments that informed societies there. He'd always attacked those who sought to defend them, even at the expense of being thought less committed to social-ism than he made out. Now no one has a word to say in favour of these forty-year-old, moribund 'people's republics'.

In Poland, Czechoslovakia, Hungary and – to a rather lesser degree – in East Germany, the traveller had been aware of a deep and pervasive cynicism. 1989 would appear to have seen, as well as the death of Communism, the death – or at least a considerable diminution – of that cynicism. And that is a cause for happiness, since, as the traveller knows from his own English life, cynicism is dangerous, the canker in any rose. It would be true to say that he does not number anyone among his friends – those who've been brought up as he has been, who've passed through the same institutions as those he's known – who is not the victim of a cynicism that eats into him.

And yet he has to remember a favourite fable of Robert Louis Stevenson, cautioning against too radical a break from the culture of one's earlier life:

> Old is the tree, and the fruit good,
> Very old and thick the wood,
> Woodman, is your courage stout?

Beware! the root is wrapped about
Your father's heart, your mother's bones,
And like the mandrake comes with groans.

Perhaps it would have been better never to have been born British, or – in his case – never to have returned to Britain, to have stayed in a society building itself up, turning its back on the past (how often his father spoke of progressive industrial relations in Germany as opposed to those in Britain poisoned by precedents), to trust the forward-carrying impulse. Or . . .

And now the bells swing the other way. It's a morning of sunshine and clear sky and light breeze. Berliners from the apartment houses opposite step blithely into the day, bound for church, a walk in the park, a visit to the East. From the East a concert comes, televised all over the world, Leonard Bernstein conducting an amalgamation of players from East and West German orchestras in a performance of Beethoven's Ninth. The *Freude* (Joy) of Schiller's Ode is changed – as the occasion seems to demand – into *Freiheit* (Freedom). Should, the traveller wonders, watching and listening in the relaxed company of his friends, this change have been made? Isn't it Joy in its intimations that spurs us on to seek Freedom, and isn't Freedom above all the condition in which we can most amply experience Joy?

As soon as the concert is finished, the news is broadcast. On the first Christmas Day that Romania has been able to celebrate since the 1940s, the National Salvation Front confirms that it has captured the Ceauşescus, who were attempting to flee the country. Bucharest, like Timisoara before it, has been a blood-bath; it's estimated that almost sixty thousand people have been killed in the fighting, and members of the Securitate are still active. There is no difference in presentation of the news between the East German channel and the West German one, just as there'd been no difference in the relaying of the festive Beethoven concert. The pictures of the Ceauşescus bring *Macbeth* eerily close; you reappreciate that the reality of that play in part derives from Shakespeare's grasp of the real events (and parallel ones) behind it. It's a little troubling, though, to find yourself enjoying the news, finding it an equally absorbing successor to Beethoven's Ninth, mood-changing but of the same momentous dimensions. Everyone has been saying how, among other things, the revolutions in Eastern Europe are a proof of the benevolent power of the Western media. The traveller himself has said this. But he's also frightened by their reductive effect on events and people. Beethoven's and Schiller's inner wrestlings, the accomplishment of musicians, the insane greed of tyrants, the brutality of thugs, the suffering of ordinary citizens and the courage of freedom fighters all are translated to enliven a comfortable room, to provide *frissons* that may or may not work more deeply into the imagination. How right Picasso was in his tribute to Guernica to portray the agonised horse with body and limbs made of newspapers.

The woods of the Tiergarten are full of people this morning; the fine weather and the palpable holiday spirit of those who walk among them make the trees today suggest their summer selves. The traveller remembers Essen's *Stadtwald* and thinks again how fitting it would be to meet – and converse with – the small boy he'd been, who'd have run down these paths, a dog at his side, in the company of these children, so very similar in appearance to himself.

They have passed – the traveller and the friend who's accompanying him – the Bauhaus Museum, and remembering what he has seen there he brings to mind the furniture of home (both Tirpitzstraße and its English successors). His parents had believed in all that – handmade, clean-lined, functional furnishing, that celebrated light and ease of movement. It was one of the many contradictions in their muddled-seeming lives: this wish, on the one hand, to purge themselves of authoritarianism, the dead hand of tradition, which was expressed in the German/German-Jewish designs they favoured, and, on the other, their nervous hope that their sons would find places for themselves in the English establishment. Looking at the Bauhaus with the park behind it, the traveller is forced to admit that contradictions are to be found in himself, as well as in his mother and father. Neither the outer structure by Gropius nor the contents of the interior (all the tables and lamps and rugs of Moholy-Nagy, Feininger, Peploe, Kandinsky – yes, even him!) have any appeal for him at all. Yet he applauds their ideals. Does this contradiction mean a far greater attachment to tradition, a far less strong desire to give himself to the forward-carrying impulse than he likes to think is the case?

It's very pleasant being with his friend of many years, talking on many subjects, and joining the cheerful, ever-changing throng as they let one path lead on to another. In the Straße des 17 Juni the queue begins – to go into East Berlin via the Brandenburger Tor; it could be as many as a hundred thousand strong, but the length of the wait does not seem to trouble those making it. The fact of being able to walk in on Christmas Day is enough to make them cheerful. And now the rule about the necessary exchange of twenty-five Deutschmarks for its equivalent in *Ostmark* has been abandoned. For one thing no one knows what the rate of exchange should be. Officially it's now put at 3:1 (whereas two days ago it was 1:1), but the relation is generally thought to be 10:1. Entry into the East is immediately succeeded by the appearance of black-marketeers in money. Guards and police look indulgently on; youths and girls working in the bureau de change regard those who – out of habit, and habit's fear – are seeking to change money the legal way with amazement. Here is yet another outward sign of inward metamorphosis. The days are not very long past when you could be dragged off to gaol for attempting black transactions.

Back on the West Berlin side of the Wall the *Mauerspechte* are even more numerous and more industrious than ever, and yet you could almost swear that there'd been no change of people, only additions to their ranks. The traveller takes more interest this time in the holes in the Wall, which do perhaps, he thinks, suggest a desire for revenge on the part of those who wrought them. The holes expose a crude but strong meshing, and you can look through this to the other side exactly as you can through the bars of a cell – on to a no man's land, empty of anything except occasional piles of rubbish: there are no *Mauerspechte* in the East.

Inevitably new slogans brighten the Western flank: the traveller notes down two in English because their ambiguities taunt him:

FIGHTING FOR GERMAN REUNION IS LIKE FUCKING
FOR VIRGINITY.

THE FUTURE'S ALWAYS UNCERTAIN, AND THE
END IS ALWAYS CLEAR.

So much of the Wallscape is ugly, so much that one apprehends from it is (even in these days of change) malign, but there is surely no corner uglier or more malign-seeming than this. Goering's Air Ministry looms up in the near distance, and the deep, dirty-red edifice called the Martin Gropius Haus, both forlorn in their bruised, gloomy grandeur. Beyond them is a sort of field of tumuli. The day is declining, the sun has gone in, the traveller is by himself. He has reached the site of the former Prinz-Albrecht-Straße, the street where the key institutions of Hitler's Third Reich were situated. Indeed he is now standing where once stood the most dreaded of them all. Prinz-Albrecht-Straße 8 was the headquarters of the Gestapo. The syllables have entered the mythology by which modern man has to steer his way.

A museum stands where the feared building once did – free, and clearly, imaginatively laid out; information is amply and assimilably given; there are constant film-shows.

It's very common to see visitors to this *Terrormuseum* leaving in tears.

The traveller enters it. He is a little reluctant to do so, since he finds almost too great an incongruity between the logical orderliness of a museum and the capitulation to the basest, cruellest urges to which the exhibits in this one testify. And can one really learn anything here? he asks himself. Haven't all our minds been glutted these last forty-odd years with images of Nazi atrocities, perhaps to the detriment of our development? They've been impedimenta for us, have overloaded our mental baggage. Perhaps – though he doesn't completely admit this to himself – he's afraid of having ceased to respond to evidence of the brutality of the regime which he – like all his generation – has read so much about.

He comes out in a troubled frame of mind. He is neither weeping nor inclined to weep. He knows instead a kind of self-despair. For what has struck at him, stunned him, is not so much the abundant revelation of human vileness but rather the presence, behind all the obscene and anti-human acts commemorated, of that quality he associated with the humanist business of running a museum: logical orderliness. Cruelties, which one supposes must have spurted forth from the perpetrators like some ejaculation of dark desire, were shown by the museum to have been built into – and therefore expected by – a system. No doubt the soldiers in Lithuania or Poland, Yugoslavia or Italy, did give vent to communal sadistic drives, but if they did, that was no more than an officialdom anticipated. There was a terrible photograph of men and women, hideously wounded, behind wire-mesh-ing, scrabbling frantically at it for relief from their pain. They were Russian, and beside the picture was a letter from HQ back in Germany: 'It has come to our attention that many of the villagers captured stumbled into the local hospital demanding help. Please see that this does not happen again.' All, clearly, had to be killed, to be seen to be dead. Gypsies, like Jews, were declared undesirable and subhuman; there-fore action had to be taken, and so the scene photographed of men setting on fire the caravan of an old and helpless gypsy was not one of spontaneous revulsion at a way of life different from the German one (though, heaven knows, that would be deplorable enough), but merely that of normal people carrying out an order normally issued. Civil servants, administrators, secretaries all collaborated in the monstrous exercise, and everyone who typed out a memo or filed a record must have known that in order for the directives to be obeyed, men would have to find in themselves the ability personally to inflict agony, humiliation and death on others. The shooting of small children, even when they're piteously holding up their hands; the experiments without anaesthetics on Jewish 'guinea-pigs'; the mass slaughter of Lithuanians compelled to kneel down in the waters of one of their own rivers – the traveller has seen many pictures of such things, and ghastly though each is, especially when taken in con-junction with its neighbours, it serves as a reminder rather than as an awakener. But the souvenirs of officialdom – these are for him this Christmas Day something else. He imagines a winter's day in Berlin – let's say forty-six years ago – and people stepping out of an office in the street that once stretched here. Ordinary work hours, ordinary home-life ahead, and yet duties will have been carried out that depend on acts of unmitigated wickedness and on the cessation of others' lives.

The museum contains mementoes of the many Germans who stood up against the Nazi regime, some of them imprisoned and condemned in the very cellars through which the tourists can now walk. Pastor Niemöller. Adam von Trott (to be hanged by piano-wire, a death that delighted Hitler so much he watched it repeatedly on film). And . . . here's a familiar face. For a minute or so the traveller cannot place him. He's handsome, rather ascetic-looking, very young, his hair unmistakably in the style of the early 1930s. It is Erich Honecker. Born in 1912, he joined the KJVD (Kommunistische Jugendverband) when he was fourteen years old; by 1930 he'd studied in the Soviet Union. When he was twenty-three years of age he was taken to Prinz-Albrecht-Straße and began his ten-year sentence, during the course of which he suffered extreme physical and psychological tortures.

Standing in the grounds of the museum, the traveller recalls Honecker's ardent, youthful face and contrasts it with the hard, closed-in countenance displayed so widely in the press these last days. For Honecker is in custody now, and will probably stand trial for corruption and treason. Treason to the ideals of socialism for which he suffered so long and so extensively. He had become another kind of prisoner, of a system which not only permitted but thrived on power – and some long-concealed weakness in his personality pushed its way upwards and flowered rankly. The youth who'd known deprivation, starvation, for his beliefs grew old and accumulated luxury cars, foreign bank accounts, is even rumoured to have been involved in the cocaine traffic.

Yet he'd once been strong enough to have no truck with the evil death-dealing machine that was Nazi Germany.

On the Wall across the way it's still just light enough to make out the slogans:

FREEDOM COMES FROM INSIDE ONESELF *BUT*
WALLS CAN STAND IN THE WAY.

FUCK ARMY OF ALL CONTRYS (*sic*)

LA ZOMBIE VOUS SALUE!

The images from the *Terrormuseum* all at once converge upon one another in some jeering dance before the eyes. There's no *sense* to be made from them, no sudden logical order ending in understanding and obliteration that can – exhibition-style – descend on them all. The traveller feels very tired, and agitated, lonely and lost (in this grim urban landscape, with no pleasingly lit home to hand) and also – yes, angry!

The wind, getting stronger now, also suggests anger. Across the tummocky ground – underneath which cells and bunkers from the Reich's last days lie – a small boy is stumbling; the traveller watches his awkward yet determined progress. He's making for *me*, he thinks, surprised.

It's too late to weep now for all the Jews, gays, gypsies, mentally infirm, physically weak, religiously zealous and 'racially impure' whom a government based in this very part of Berlin wanted to vilify, repudiate, and destroy with the maximum pain. But he can salute the representatives of all these groups that coexist inside him, and inside everybody.

Thinking this is also to understand that yet another wall has been dismantled, the wall between the years.

# Two

The sharp wind makes the traveller's eyes water, and maybe that's causing them to deceive him. For the child who's just arrived beside him, fair-haired, blue-eyed, a little stocky, and scarved against the winter weather, seems to him his past self. And the moan of the wind blowing across the barren site of Prinz-Albrecht-Straße sounds in his ears as that child addressing him – articulate beyond his age, and speaking, not as he'd expected him to in German, but in English.

The small boy says: 'I know that expression on your face; it's the one you see on just about everybody's face after a visit to the museum. Shock, incredulity, even after all these years, after almost half a century of bombardment with information. And you look angry too. Are you angry with the Germans, with humanity in general, with . . . ?'

The traveller makes himself interrupt. 'At this very moment,' he replies, 'I'm angry with *you*.'

'With me?'

'Yes; I've let you dominate me too much. That you saw dreadful things in the Germany of the Occupation, that you suffered there – yourself and on other people's behalf – of course I recognise. But you've never sufficiently released me, and consequently I've failed in perspective. Museums like this one force me to acknowledge truths you've tried to keep away from me. Obviously in the years since we parted I've informed myself of the dreadful drama of the Devil's Decade and the war in Europe. But thanks to *you*, there's always been, in the forefront of my mind, the destruction of the German cities as – so to speak – the final, the culminating act of the whole tragedy. I resent that.'

'Do you mean,' says the small boy, 'that you accuse yourself of not facing up to the question of German guilt? That you've allowed what I saw in Essen, in Bochum and Dortmund and Düsseldorf and Köln, to obscure that issue?'

'That comes into it, certainly,' answers the traveller. 'There's a passage in Thomas Mann's *Doctor Faustus* that I always remember, which describes a group of Germans in an air-raid shelter; many of them felt they'd brought the terror from the skies upon themselves. After all, who bombed Guernica in April 1937? Who in September 1939 let hell fall down upon Polish cities, Warsaw in particular? The Germans!'

The small boy says in a low, almost pleading voice: '*I* knew Matthias, you seem to forget. It wasn't really so very different to deduce what *he* had done, that he'd been as "bad" as the British when they pounded the Ruhr. But that didn't mean that I ever changed my feelings about what had happened in the places I knew, that it ceased to seem an atrocity. I kept questioning and protesting right up to the last days in Germany.'

'Isn't that what I'm complaining about?' The traveller tries to keep exasperation and self-reproach out of his voice. 'That the intensity of your response has hindered a, shall we say, more comprehensive approach to the subject? When I was growing up and finding out more and more about the recent history I was heir to, I used to get annoyed at my (our) father for his endless attempts to exonerate the Germans. Because he loved German culture so much, because he had so many close relationships with Germans, it was anathema to him to blame Germany for almost anything. I don't know whether you were present or not at those Sunday lunch-times when he'd go on and on about the undermining of Weimar, the intransigence of Clemenceau, the behaviour of the French in the Ruhr, the exaction of reparations payments that everyone knew the crippled German republic couldn't afford, and so on. I got fed up with it, not because I disputed the facts, and even less because I doubted their importance, but because my father insisted on concentrating on one aspect of the case rather than on the case as a whole. And also because there was too much emotional investment in its presentation. My father – in this respect, anyway – was a good person; not the most minuscule part of him had any sympathy for Hitler's Reich at all. But by giving so much of his powers of understanding to the humiliated Germans of the 1920s, he did end up – externally, at any rate – carrying out a sort of whitewashing exercise.

'I – you have seen to it! – have been guilty in much the same way. We must remember that people know us (and are influenced by us) largely by what we do, say and write, even though we may unconsciously suggest our doubts, our secret mental lives. When the subject of Germany and the war presents itself – as it does almost daily; fifty years and we are still grappling with its demands – I, sooner or later, return to the destruction of the German cities. In all their ghastliness they continually obtrude, and then I can't think straight. Years of education, of *self*-education, are invalidated by the pressures you still exert on me.'

The small boy looks sad. 'I'm sorry you should feel like this,' he says, 'and I must say I can't help thinking what you've just said is both a misuse and a betrayal of me.

'First of all, I didn't *choose* Essen rather than Guernica or Warsaw; chance made that German city my experience, and I reacted accordingly. No doubt if my earliest memories had been of bombed Warsaw my focus on the whole explosion of Europe would indeed be different. But it seems a bit much to expect everyone to be born at convenient vantage-points in time and place, from which great historical panoramas can unfold. No doubt what I saw has conditioned you, conditioned your responses to many things, and your absorption of certain facts. That doesn't diminish the sufferings that Essen, and Germany as a whole, showed me and that have lived on in you. Nor does it diminish the validity of my/our experiences. For one thing they weren't unique. By trying to downplay them in some attempt to gain perspective, you're also downplaying their representative nature, and therefore the bewilderments and difficulties of many others such as you.

'I feel misused because you don't seem to have drawn from me – at least not as you present yourself at this meeting – the truth that what is horrible in one context is horrible in another. Horrible is perhaps too much *my* sort of word, a small child's. Let's not be afraid of using the term "evil".

'You spoke of Guernica, and when you look at the course of events on our continent from before the outbreak of war to its fearful last days, Guernica does seem to be the first of its own peculiar victims – now part of your consciousness, your world-picture. That April day in 1937, and the ancient Basque city, with the old tree under which the first Basque parliament met, and all the men and women going to market, and the Germans shattering the place with bombs, including those people making their way marketwards. "They bombed and bombed and bombed," said the Mayor afterwards. Evil erupted in triumphant, utterly naked form.

'And then we move on to the end of the war. As you say, there are almost *too* many examples to take, and I saw a good many of them, so why don't we think of Wuppertal, since it's a town of personal significance, since "our" brother was born there? The whole area had already been pounded almost into obliteration, but in one of the last major raids of all they unleashed a new weapon on Wuppertal. In August 1943 the British had used on Hamburg phosphorus incendiary bombs that melted streets and created rivers of flame (almost two hundred thousand people in Hamburg were killed in the bombing, you may remember). Well, on Wuppertal *liquid* phosphorus was dropped. Hundreds of people became like torches and ran to the river Wupper to try to put themselves out; it was low-target bombing so those up in the planes knew perfectly well what they were doing. (Your mother alluded to this war crime, you remember.)

'So tell me what the difference is between Guernica and

**171**

Wuppertal, either with regard to its victims or – perhaps more important in the argument that seems to be developing between us – its perpetrators? Both are instances of yielding to evil, of serving it. If the one horrifies you, the other does. I'd looked to you to see these intolerable happenings as both the same and as individual causes for grief, not for you to join them up in some causal line. They *can* be so joined, I'm not disputing that, but we are – both of us, you as much as me – *post-war* people. The conflagration that was Europe should have made us all put the ghastliness of the raids way above any consideration of deed, reprisal, result. When I lived in Essen I refused – to the very end – to put myself in the position of *anyone*, whatever nationality, who took part in deathly warfare because I thought it was entering the cast of mind of the Devil. You can't have forgotten how, when I got to England, I would never read war-stories of the Biggles type, never play war-games. I'd seen the ruins, and I knew that whatever was said to the contrary, only wicked emotions could have attended their making. That sense of indignation which I left you seems to have weakened.'

'So that's the misuse? What about the betrayal?' says the traveller, after a pause.

The small boy gives a wry smile. 'We ignorant innocents see each person as charged with significance; the process of having to think in terms of groups, countries is a hard, fraught one. To me the fact that the men who rained bombs on Guernica and those who jumped into the River Wupper as human torches were *different* is so obvious it doesn't need saying. But it clearly does. Of the people who died in Wuppertal, how many had any control whatever over events?

How many of them even had real convictions or consecutive thoughts about Germany, its policies, its destiny and so on? A few, who repeated what the government had told them, a few more who obediently did what it said. Many of those burned up were children and animals incapable of any "German" thought or action, and who had quite definitely not even heard of Guernica. Just to bear them in mind for a few minutes is first of all to make the idea of attack morally untenable, second to render wholly ridiculous the use of the word "German" or "Germany" – in this context anyway. As if you could tie up complex organisms in time and geography. A small child and a dog know terror and pain and desolation as much as a general or a professor. And a *German* child and a *German* dog are as much, or as little, German as that master-minding general or that propagandising professor. And yet the term "Germany" is not to include them, it would appear.'

The traveller attempts a mocking, adult smile. 'Are you trying to tell me that when I hear the name of a country with an aggressive government, I should make myself think of all the small children and dogs inside it?'

The small boy's blue eyes turn grey as they're apt to when he's indignant, or serious, or both. 'Why not?' he says. 'In fact you would be thinking of a far greater number than you would if you thought of those possessed of political opinion and power. And another thing –'

'Yes?'

'Almost no one is possessed wholly by a policy. Think of what a complex world *I* was – uncomprehending yet deductive, intelligent and also stupid, fearful yet also often joyful,

**173**

ecstatically happy. Think what a complex world *you* are, though you're determined on trying to simplify it, or so it seems to me. The man delivering fire – and death-by-fire – to Basques, German soldiers, Vietcong, is giving himself to the Devil, but the Devil is not, as we know, all-supreme. And before the surrender, think of all that man has been and known. In him the whole universe has its being. Kill him even after his cruelties, and you're still killing a world.'

'So you advocate never killing in any circumstances?' The traveller is already a little weary of the discussion; he's had versions of it with so many friends over the years, at school, at Oxford, in pubs, at dinner-tables.

The child's voice rises as it did in the tempers he occasionally threw at Tirpitzstraße. 'I'm not advocating. I'm saying what I couldn't do. If you choose to let your memories of my years in Essen be swallowed up by other people's facts, opinions, ideas, experiences, so be it. I can't help feeling disappointed by the renunciation of what was given you to witness and empathise with, but it's not exactly uncommon. But I might as well put it in terms that could make an appeal to you. It's only luck that Toni, Trude, Günter, Hannelore, Matthias, Klaus, Dr Ahlens, Finette and Achim weren't all either crushed under falling walls or consumed by those fires. That apparently is acceptable to you?'

'Of course not!' says the traveller. 'You know how I've preserved them all in my mind and heart – for forty years. Even Finette whom I had reasons for disliking – somehow (those letters of hers I once found!) she's transcended the situation of Tirpitzstraße 49; I can appreciate her. How can you accuse me of being indifferent to their survival?' He can feel, for all his so much greater superiority in years, the pricking of tears behind his eyes. 'Toni, for instance. I've been thinking about her a lot recently, partly because I often see people who look a bit like her in Berlin. (Though she must be almost eighty now.) Saying goodbye to her on Essen station and realising, as I see it now, all the sacrifices she'd made for me, all the jealousies she'd banished because I had so much more than her daughter or her friends' children . . . all that's *my* experience more than it's yours, because it grows with you as you grow into life.' It isn't the afternoon's cold wind that's making his eyes water now. 'And she used to write us letters when we were back in England: she said that our names were written in her heart's blood. Those were her exact words!'

'And,' says the small boy, 'as we've said in another context, every case is both the same as others and its individual self. Toni is (or was) Toni. But she's in one important sense no different from lots of Tonis who did not survive the inferno that each German town became. What a Toni was to you, what a Toni was to herself – no one has the right to eliminate it for any reason whatever. That's what I would have thought – what I *did* think, except the whole notion of making war was so mysterious to me. But you – well, you haven't been so very faithful to me, so perhaps I should expect that in this respect you have,' he gives a rather contemptuous little smile, 'grown beyond me!'

How ugly their surroundings are, as evening darkens the wastes and almost random-seeming buildings of this part of Berlin. Evening does not beautify the Wall, while reducing the impact of its graffiti; the hillocks that hide the former torture chambers are humps of cold shadow: it's not hard to think of death as something malicious here. The great pile, the colour of rotten plums, of Goering's Air Ministry casts a forbidding shadow on the waste-ground around it. Even in the lights coming on in the near distance it's hard to find promises of home and home's simulacra.

The conversation seems to have come to a sort of (not very satisfactory) end, and the traveller moves on. He'll walk on, pulling his coat tighter round him against the bite of evening, and stop at one of the booths at the edge of the bare expanse of the Potsdamer Platz. Now that it's a two-way entry point, that corner seems to warrant its little posts of commercial pleasure a little more. It'd be nice to have a glass of hot, spiced *Glühwein*, the perfect drink for cold dusk in winter.


The small boy is running to catch up with him. I suppose I have *not* been as faithful to him as I should have been, he thinks (a little despite himself, for hasn't he mostly *not* violated his conscience?). The child of Bredeney didn't hide his emotions, his beliefs; if he disliked or disapproved, he cried, he got angry, he made himself objectionable by insolence or not eating or even flailing out. His successor put very much greater store on being amiable, on accommodating himself. Wasn't it inevitable, this loss of purity? You turned into a St Sebastian at some stage of your development, assailed by arrows from every direction; you learned the position to adopt to receive the least, and the least painful, of these. Otherwise you were done for . . .

'You remember the *Kasperltheater*?' the boy is asking now,

panting a little as he catches up with the middle-aged man. (In the distance the tap-tapping, the chip-chipping can be heard. The traveller resalutes the new species, to which vicariously he feels he belongs: a *Mauerspecht* would listen to a babbling child, would not despise him for simplicity, for over-intentness. A *Mauerspecht* would not be impressed by a plenitude of rational arguments based on what other people had done or thought; they wished to do and think and *feel* for themselves.)

'You remember the *Kasperltheater*?' the boy repeats.

'Yes, how couldn't I? There are folk-toys in the museum here, which reminded me of them – though there's no collection here to match the puppet-museum in Munich.' (The traveller thinks of the visit he made to the Münchner Stadtmuseum, whose curator had been so friendly to him, of its superb assembly of marionettes and glove puppets, from all over the world and all over Germany including Westfalen, which had made not only his own childhood but those of countless others almost tangibly close to him.)

'There were always the *Hexe* and the *Gespenst* to be taken into account, weren't there? Can't you still see the *Hexe* with her asymmetrical eyes and malevolent mouth, and the *Gespenst* with his white death's-head? Haven't you felt their power ever since we parted company, you and I, felt them at school, in Northern Ireland when Ian Paisley addressed his supporters, among *franquistas* at the time of the attempted *golpe* in Spain, 1981, among racists of the American Deep South and vicious frontier guards of the DDR, amid all the hysterical clamour of the Falklands War? But always – as in the *Kasperltheater* – you've been able to set in contrast to

177

them, outshining them, as it were, the king (*der König*) with his golden crown and bright eyes and silver beard. That's how I imagined God to be . . .'

'And that's *still* how I imagine Him to be,' the traveller observes a little bitterly. 'I've never been able to substitute any other image; as if those bright eyes are watching us all, and that scarlet cloak can be thrown over the whole world.

'Not,' he adds hastily, 'that that's how intellectually I . . .'

'Yes, yes, yes,' the child cuts in, rather ruthlessly for one so young. 'You aren't so stupid, are you, that you think that that's how even a child *intellectually* envisages God?'

In the darkling space between the mounds and the old Nazi Air Ministry the king abruptly and illuminatingly appears. And, recalls the traveller:

DER GOTT DER MENSCHEN IST AUCH DER GOTT
DER TIERE.

'The point I'm trying to make,' persists the child, all but tugging at the traveller's coat now, 'is that the king is always there, just as he was in the *Kasperltheater*. His very presence nullifies the *Hexe* and the *Gespenst*, even though they don't go away. There's no need to fall into their ways to defeat them; we only have to keep the king in mind constantly, and they will be shown up – at some time or other – in all their hideousness and sterility.'

'Easier said than done!' says the traveller, and those photographs from the Terror Museum beset his mind's eye – the helmeted, jackbooted soldiers shooting young Lithuanians in the stream, the gypsies' caravan being set alight, the small bewildered child putting up his hands to surrender to men determined to kill him . . .

'Obviously!' says the small boy. 'It's strange, isn't it, that you, who've seen so much more of the world than I have, judge things by whether they're easy or not. *I* – pampered child that I was, with a *domestique* bringing me hot chocolate every morning, and, whatever grim sights I'd seen, a pleasant house always to return to – did *not* expect this. I knew it would get me into trouble – and earn worried looks and babble about a "trick cyclist" – if I continued with my questions. Yet I did. Anyway they weren't questions really. They were protests.'

'Maybe,' says the traveller, and the exasperation he's already given expression to, at the omnipresence of this small boy and his years in Essen, surges up within him anew, 'maybe, but we inhabit different – well, *worlds* really, you and I. What holds good for you doesn't for me.'

The child gave a perhaps ill-judged sarcastic little laugh. Ill-judged because laughter is never likely to woo an opponent, let alone make him change.

'You don't understand then why you've come to Berlin now? You – and one or two hundred thousand others?'

The traveller recalls his recent thoughts.

'I'm a very great deal more likely to know the answer to that than you are.' And he quickens his footsteps: the child is a nuisance now. Hasn't – reflects the traveller – something very like guilt compelled him to keep an unflagging watch over the interrelationships of European countries – even to the point of distancing himself from his own because of Thatcher's rabid isolationism? 'I'd have thought,' he says, 'that it's political concern that has brought me – and all these others – to Berlin, but that is hardly something a small boy like you could understand.'

It's surely possible that this petulant snub may dissolve the child into the air as speedily as he manifested himself out of it. But in fact he is keeping pace, with some dignity, and his high voice has a singular self-confidence.

'I don't think you've all come for political reasons,' he says, 'and I could almost prove it. It's impossible for so many to have the same ideas or interpretations of what's been going on in Eastern Europe, and many of them won't ever have taken great interest in the concerns of those countries, probably won't even now be very well informed or clear about past situations there. Even less will they have given – or will they give – detailed attention to the implications of what's been happening, the tangled economic problems, the equally knotty ones of international law. But that doesn't alter the deep feeling that they all share, that's uniting them all.

'What they're really celebrating is the fact that human beings can stand up to tyrannous systems without violence, without resort to, let's use the language that's dear to me – may I call them still the *Hexe* and the *Gespenst*?' He shoots a sharp glance at the traveller. 'Don't overstress my ignorance,' he remarks. 'I'm aware that without the consent, either tacit or explicit, of the Soviet Union and the realities behind that consent (of little to no endorsement of governments not put there by free voting), these demonstrations wouldn't have occurred. But that isn't by any means contrary to what I'm in the process of saying, since the felt, unacted hostility to authoritarianism played a major part in the Russian decisions. What's made us all – after what seems an eternity of not being able to do so – *rejoice* in being human is the fact that their protests took the form of simply presenting themselves – as flesh-and-blood sentient beings. Together. In large numbers. In the places designed for people to meet, to assemble, *their* places.

'Their non-violence had taken the most extraordinary courage. It always does. Think of 9 October in Leipzig. Demonstrations in East Berlin had been dealt with by the authorities with great brutality, protesters being beaten senseless by the police in full public view. By that evening a great many people were pretty sure that the rumours that Honecker had authorised the use of live ammunition on crowds were quite true. That Sunday the Bishop in the St Niklauskirche, who sympathised with the reformers, begged the Leipzigers to respect their own lives. So the fifty thousand who entered the Karl Marx Platz must have done so with every expectation of beatings, indeed of shootings. Perhaps something emanating from them, with their "No Violence" cries and attitudes *did* work its power on authority. Perhaps the image of the good king that all held together, great and shining, within their minds did loom forth from the protesters and cast a transfiguring light . . . *Wir sind das Volk!* Being human, being there to see and touch and hear and smell, that was enough. Each person was a *Kasperltheater* whose cast contained a king.

'Later on – well, not so very much later on – the demonstrations grew, as you know, to even greater proportions. Who was the victor? Not so much Neues Forum and its associates, but the king in the human *Kasperlspiel*, the wisdom

181

inside us, the gentleness that's profoundly natural to us, our perpetual need, and ability, to transcend the demands of expediency and greed. And *that's* why you're in Berlin now – you and all those countless others. A point has been made, just as you were despairing of the very truth it proves.'

As he finds the path that edges along the wall to the Potsdamer Platz the traveller thinks: This child, in telling me off for not being faithful to him, doesn't know perhaps the extent of my disloyalty.

Not answering him – in fact, does his little speech *require* an answer? – he brings to mind all the times he's been tempted to renounce him. The small boy in Tirpitzstraße 49 has not particularly appealed to him. As he surrendered to the ethos of his English schools, and acquired their habits – some of them maybe appealing to a self he'd left behind in Worcestershire during his German years – he came a little to despise the over-fastidious, introverted non-combatant that Essen had known. He would have liked a more assertive – why not say it? – robuster-seeming earlier self, and also possibly a merrier one. The child may now say that he cherished the domain of the king and repudiated always that of the *Hexe* and the *Gespenst*, but it sometimes struck him that his abhorrence of violence and its consequences had led him to inhabit a shadowland, an interior place all haunted and isolating, which was very much kin to some of *their* domains.

The traveller's English education had led him to mistrust that broodiness, that inwardness (which also made him see outward things as projections, as realisations of inner qualities, spiritual forces). He came to set store by the active, even the practical – which gave a harder edge still to the judgements he exercised on others, and, most of all, upon himself. Yet the actions of his own that he most valued were always enactments of dramas that had occurred, even split seconds before, within, and which were themselves assemblages of deeper elements still.

The young fellow he'd like to have been – whose indignation at deeds he didn't approve of took the form of vigorous invective or explosions and which didn't inhibit a giving to life, an enthusiastic entering into things, into the hurlyburly and the humdrum – had, he thought, joined up with him for a while. In his student days, his early manhood, he had opinions, purposes, ideals even, which he acted upon; the energy he felt daily within his body took him to friendships, to social life, to sex . . .

When did all this stop? Physically he is stronger than he's ever been, mentally his powers of concentration are greater. He can tackle new and difficult tasks from which he'd have shrunk in youth. And yet . . . he is possessed by a restlessness, a discontent, a sadness, which has indeed brought that child of Tirpitzstraße much closer to him, even before this encounter on the site of Prinz-Albrecht-Straße.

NOT TELLIG THE TRUOTH. What a crime that had seemed to him! A crime that had hit him because he knew it was everywhere practised around him. He had wanted to penetrate behind the surfaces of the world that he was faced with – and had known that doing so would be terrible.

So; the traveller has now to give in, to sigh and admit that he would, could never have been otherwise: that what lay imprisoned in the ruins and in the suburbs of Essen did not admit of an alternately merry and challenging child. As his

**183**

former self had reminded him, tartly, only minutes back, he had not chosen his time, his place; he had been confronted with monuments to the *Hexe* and the *Gespenst*, to their appalling capacities, to a *Kasperlspiel* which had accorded them the major roles. Only a shrinking from them, only a determination not to pretend that this hadn't been so, and to believe, however confusedly, in some restoration of the scarlet-cloaked king – only these ways were open to him.

And now?

He feels that the small boy has somehow read his thoughts (isn't that really how and why they've been able to meet up?) and is embarrassed, perhaps a little repentant. He feels rather than hears the question he's asking of him. 'Haven't you ever felt proud of me, then? Haven't you ever said, "I'm glad I was the child Tirpitzstraße knew"?'

He's alone again now. Well, in the sense of being without that fair-haired, blue-eyed boy who could, everyone said, be either English or German. A van is driving down the wide, gravelled way, and from its loudspeaker horn comes a voice unmistakably from London, twangy, a little nasal, cheery: 'British Sector. A very happy Christmas to you all. British Sector, a very happy Christmas to you all.'

There are many people crowding round the booths. More postcards to buy: BERLIN – AN DER MAUER, showing an East Berliner and a West Berliner meeting on top of the newly cleared Wall; WIR SIND DAS VOLK, with two pictures of the crowds in East Berlin, in the Alexander-Platz on 4 November 1989 and on 9 November 1989 in the very capitalist heart of West Berlin, the Ku'damm. T-shirts with I WAS HERE ON 9 NOVEMBER; mugs; pencils; caps; posters. And then other things to buy – a group of East Berlin youths are laughingly clustered round one stand. It is selling condoms, all with facetious (English) names: 'Snake-charmer', 'Gamekeeper', 'Racing Motorist', 'Beginner', 'Economist', 'Freshfruit-drinker', 'Traffic Warden', 'Motor Cyclist', 'Postman'.

Just like the graffiti on the Wall nearby the words, taken together, form a song to capitalist, exploitative, consumerist sex, a song that seems to be going down very well indeed . . .

The traveller treats himself to *Glühwein*; Berlin is lighting up, the swoops of the Philharmonie, the phallic soaring of the victory column above the now dark woods, and – moving your head the other way – the charmless office and apartment blocks of the Eastern city. Yes, he tells himself, I'd have liked to have told the child that there was a time when I was pleased with him, one time when I consciously saluted him across the years.

# Three

And though the child eludes him (swallowed up by the Potsdamer Platz, it seems), the traveller continues to address him during his tramp back to the centre of West Berlin, answering that question he may or may not have asked.

'I wonder why you didn't appear to me *then*? Why you've chosen Berlin and not the Essen you lived in as your place of confrontation with me?

'I wonder also why I took so long to return to the city of my – of *your* – early years. I visited Germany many times in my twenties and thirties, and not once did I attempt to go back to the Ruhr. I went often to Frankfurt, where a branch of our family comes from, I paid several visits to Stuttgart, and it was in a Stuttgart garden – standing beside someone I felt deeply for – that I knew one of those tweaks at the curtains of conventional Time. I was in the middle of a beauti-fully laid-out fruit garden, a sort of vegetable geometry of currant-bushes and raspberry canes, and for a moment the years parted and I felt not only that Tirpitzstraße 49 was at hand, but also some significant disclosure about my life there, and my life since. And also maybe about the nature of my relationship with Michael, dark, sensuous, partly Jewish. Michael picked me bunches of red currants, and the moment passed away. But even then I never thought of journeying on to Essen. It wouldn't have been difficult after all.

'No, I'd turned forty before I made the decision, really very suddenly, that I must see Essen again. I was living in Spain. Perhaps *you* can explain why – in, I should say, 1978 – a restlessness took hold of me that has still not let me go. My detestation and disapproval of the Thatcher government later fuelled it; bent on insularity, it needed, so I argued, to be offset by immersion in other countries, cultures, by acting out my internationalism. But I know that the urge to become the "traveller" predates Mrs Thatcher's first victory, though it's conceivable I read the signs of her ascendancy before it was electorally manifested. America, France, Spain, Italy, the Netherlands – I've lived and worked in them all, until I truly feel I have a home nowhere.

'You, cushioned in Tirpitzstraße, didn't know, except vicariously through observation of German children, what it meant to worry about money, about living conditions. You will perhaps never acknowledge that you were able to develop your feeling life so amply because of the material comfort of your external life, but it's true. I, of course, am your beneficiary. But from 1978 onwards I've put other things before security; with no money of my own, and earning really very little through writing and teaching, I've lived rather precariously, certain only that I'd survive the immediate future. What I'll think about it all later I'm not sure; at this moment I know that I've had no alternative. I've been driven on by forces I didn't – and don't – understand. That's why I find it easy to imagine a new human species like the *Mauerspechte* coming into being. That's why I can empathise with all those East Germans who've felt compelled to cross into the West – whether via Hungary, Czechoslovakia, or their own frontier. Viewed rationally, in the light of the now almost certain reunification of Germany, their emigration may today seem ill-judged, pointless. But they couldn't *not* make it.

'In 1981 I moved to Spain where I stayed for two years. The Spain of that time filled me with emotions similar to those I feel when I confront the Eastern Europe of today; it was a society in transformation, moving from autocracy to democracy, and incredulous and delighted at the changes that almost every month seemed to bring. Witnessing the atmosphere of the *golpe*, of the *franquista* demonstrations for the sixth anniversary of the Caudillo's death, of the Tejero trial, you appreciated the fragility of the new Spain, but also its strength, the will of people who'd decided to live more abundantly, to accept the complexity of the human personality both in themselves and in others. For me Spain was an exhilarating experience; every part of my being felt permeated by the prevalent optimism. So perhaps it was Spain which gave me the confidence to face the scenes of my (your) past.

'I remember the very hour when I knew that I would revisit Essen. It was midsummer; I was working in Segovia, that city which stands in the barren *meseta* rather like a moored ship. In the heart of the old city, the Plaza Mayor, you could sit in the evening, when the oppressive heat abated a bit, and watch the storks who nest on the roof-tops of the old quarter winging their way to the pinnacles and spires of the cathedral. I never grew tired of this strange spectacle; the sun went down, and then about an hour later storks – ungainly but somehow very impressive – made for these posts which they'd occupy until dawn, becoming like figures – gargoyles – carved out of stone. What fascinated me was that there was never any competition for a place; the storks seemed to know just where vacancies would be, seemed to have arrived at an understanding of how many birds per night the cathedral pinnacles could accommodate. The stork, I remembered from the Bible, has his appointed times – the whole mysterious business of migration illustrated that. And I realised that *my* appointed time to go back to my former German home had arrived, that it was, in a sense, waiting for me, just as pinnacles were seemingly waiting for these storks. The very next day I bought my ticket. When my work ended the next week, I would journey from central Spain by bus to the Ruhrgebiet.'


As he, in his imagination, says all this to the invisible child, he can see – momentarily eclipsing these busy Berlin streets – the desert country of canyons and rock castles that stretches between Madrid and Zaragoza, and remembers how, preparing for the assault of personal memories, involving the unkindness of people one to another, he had felt a profound gratitude to this empty, uninhabitable land. The bus was full, for the most part, of Spanish *Gastarbeiter* returning to Germany, outwardly cheerful but clearly also sad to be leaving behind friends and families and the intimately familiar.

A night's journey and then they found themselves in the dewy, wooded mountains of the Vosges – in Alsace.

Germany, after these Spanish and French landscapes, seemed far too populous, to wear its industry with a curious nakedness, just as an insect's body often exposes all its workings. For all the sculptured serenity of the German countryside, it gave you no way of forgetting what kept the wheels of modern life turning and turning, no respite from realising the sources of your money.

'I had to change buses in Frankfurt and it was dark by the time I arrived in Cologne. So of my journey to the heart of the Ruhr I could see very little.

'I probably should tell you something that I don't think will astonish you. Not only have I never forgotten the house in Bredeney, I have visited it in my mind virtually every day of my life. Whenever I read a novel (or indeed anything else which requires envisaging both the interior and garden of an "ordinary" house), I place it there, unless given very particular descriptions that make doing so utterly wrong. And when I have to imagine somewhere grander, well, I go in my mind to the Villa Hügel.

'So, for more than three decades Tirpitzstraße 49 had been a place of emotional and psychic encounters. Friends didn't believe me when I said I could recall every feature of it. And I began to agree with them, to think that I had fashioned out of a real house – far back in my past – a Platonic one. No wonder I was decidedly nervous at the return; no wonder that when I saw, flashing by on the motorway, a sign saying BREDENEY, my heart beat very fast, and I could hardly credit the place with external existence.

'The centre of Essen – not that I'd expected much of it – was almost alarming in its predictable anonymity. I could have been – so it seemed at that hour of night – almost anywhere on two continents; the streets existed for only one human species – the shopper – who, after a certain hour, vanishes.

'I hadn't even reserved a hotel.

'I saw a young couple just outside the bus station, and asked them if they knew how long it would take to get to Bredeney by public transport, and if there were hotels there. They said that they didn't know, but that the girl's father, an old resident of Essen, would. He'd come to meet them off the bus, and was even now sitting in that car over there. He was sure to know . . .

'What was it about the tall, lean man with his untidy silvery hair that made me feel immediately able to tell him my real reason for returning to Essen? What was it about the way I told my story that made him respond by driving me all the way out to Bredeney himself? But Tirpitzstraße – no, he didn't know it. But it would be in the street-guide, doubtless.

'It wasn't. I felt a stab of panic. How could it not be? Was this going to be the first indication that I had *created* those German years that haunted me so much, that I had made mistake after mistake about them, starting with the name of my former street – or perhaps with locating it in Bredeney . . . The tall elderly man – wasn't there something of Dr Ahlens about him? – said, as it was getting quite late, I must give priority to finding a hotel. He knew one, near to

191

the Villa Hügel. And with his pronouncing that once so familiar name, self-confidence returned.

'At the hotel my new friend inquired of the receptionist the whereabouts of a Tirpitzstraße, not to be found on the street plan. "Wasn't it one of the streets which changed its name?" she said, her words giving the inanimate strange powers of decision-making. More than likely, said the man, after all a martial name like Tirpitz would hardly be acceptable to the builders of the new, non-militaristic Germany. He would try and find out for me the name the road now went under, and would telephone me mid-morning next day.

'This he did – but I had already found my old home.'


The traveller turns round to see whether the child is listening, is impressed, but of course, he isn't there. The shops in the Tauenzienstraße are shut, but certain cafés and bars are open – and so are the booths with their stacks of festive produce. Surely the child would like to hear how he'd woken up to the freshness and fulness of the late-June morning – *in his own German city* – and had decided to go for a walk? Pleasant houses stood in pleasant gardens; you would envisage for those who lived in them a completely trouble-free past. Only the domestic virtues were testified to here; any ideals of *Vaterland* or military glory seemed ludicrously inapposite.

As he walked, a sense of knowledge possessed him. Of course he'd been along these residential roads before – many, many times. Knowledge was not so much in his head as in his feet, his eyes, his nose. And in this particular road the information that seems, unasked-for, to have returned to them is the most pressing of all. Use it, his members urged: doesn't this bend, this double row of trees, mean anything to you?

' "That house over there," I said to myself, "that's very like our home." Creeper-covered walls, and windows placed exactly as ours were. Then, crossing over the road, my whole body – or so it felt – addressed me. Said: This *is* your old home.

'And sure enough it was No. 49.

'There was no sign of activity in it. This being a fine summer day its occupants were doubtless away on a holiday. The longer I confronted its façade the surer I was. And yet – how could I prove it? All I knew so far was that Tirpitzstraße no longer existed.

'In the small front garden of the next-door house I saw a woman watching me. No doubt my extreme curiosity was making *her* curious. She approached me – not very diffidently – and asked if I wanted anything. She was, I should say, in her early seventies, but very healthy and strong-looking, with fair, sun-bleached hair and tanned skin, and large, light-blue eyes.

'I explained my situation. That I was sure I'd come back to my former home. That I would like enormously to go inside . . . "The owners are on holiday," she said, and my heart sank. "But they return at midday. And *why* are you so sure?" I tried to stammer out reasons. I didn't say that my limbs, my senses, had preserved this place for me, and were testifying on its behalf now . . .

' "Perhaps you'd better come inside my house," the woman said, "and you can peep into their garden and see

**193**

whether you're right." But though no response could surely be more friendly than this quite spontaneous invitation, friendliness was not what she suggested, with her rather cold smile and intense eyes. Nevertheless I was very pleased to follow her into what I now knew to be the one-time home of that little dark-haired playmate of mine, Hilary.

'I perhaps don't need to tell you that when, from this woman's terrace, I looked into the next-door garden, my body's memories were vindicated. The garden was as I had pictured it all these years, with one omission.

' "There was, I thought, a magnolia-tree," I said.

' "Yes, a beautiful one; *I* planted it," the woman said. "It got a kind of illness, and had to be cut down last year. Such a pity!"

'My pleasure at knowing that I was right, that if not precisely back in my old home, I was gazing upon a part of it, was cut into by the strange words, "*I* planted it".

' "Did you say that *you* planted the magnolia-tree?" I asked.

' "Indeed! And I suppose at this point I should put your mind at rest and say yes, this *was* Tirpitzstraße. My husband and I bought both these houses before the war; we lived in one, my mother in another. It was our home till the Occupation, till your parents requisitioned it."

'The words sent dismay speeding through me. I had never ever thought how we came to be in our house! I had never thought of the Germans who, so obviously, must have been living in it till . . . till my father's arrival in advance of my mother and myself.

' "I don't think that my parents . . ."

' "They didn't personally turn me out, no! Obviously not! But that's what it amounted to, wasn't it? That's what it felt like. Oh, yes, I remember your mother and father – what they looked like – and you too, come to that. Let me tell you this: those years you were all here in my houses, my mother and I – my husband had been killed – had a very, *very* horrible time. Living among the ruins of central Essen. Oh, but you perhaps don't remember how it was. You were only a small child."

'Perhaps something on my face told her that she was wrong. I *did* remember, had never ceased to remember. Could she see me trying to place her in some "hole" in the rubble such as Matthias and his family had once occupied? Her expression changed, and so did her tone of voice. "Well, it's all a long time ago," she said. "We're not enemies any more."

'The word "enemies" – so charged, so anachronistic – startled me. This was the vocabulary of Philip and Elspeth which my parents had told me to reject.

'She offered me some coffee, and suggested that I went round later that evening to No. 49. She was sure the people who lived there now would be pleased to see me.

'I returned to the hotel in time to receive the telephone call from my friend of the night before. He reconfirmed the knowledge I now had – told me again Tirpitzstraße's new name, honouring a philanthropist famous for his rescue work among the Jewish communities.

'All day as I visited the Villa Hügel and its grounds, walked down to the Baldeneysee through that beech-wood cut through by a ravine, I pondered over the evacuation of the

German inhabitants of Bredeney and the moving into their houses of British people such as my parents. What scenes of lamentation had attended this process? Certainly the lady I'd been talking to had nurtured her resentment all her cold, hungry years. She had saved enough money to buy back one of her two former houses when the Bundesrepublik was set up and it became possible for Germans to buy back their old property. Questions came into my mind: Had Toni or Trude worked for her before my parents? Old Peter the gardener certainly must have done. Though I have a good memory, I could not recall a single remark anyone had made about our predecessors in the house. They'd never been given a thought.

'Somehow this seemed all too emblematic of so many aspects of our lives. We live at the expense of people we have consigned to the unknowable, the unmentionable. We are all occupiers, guilty of the crimes inherent in any occupation. . .'

By now he's reached streets of domestic dwellings which are kin to those of Essen. The brashness and opulence of the Ku'damm are replaced now by citadels of burgher *Gemütlichkeit*.

It's fitting enough surroundings for the conclusion of his story. (He still hasn't told the child how and why he was – for once – proud of him. But he intends to, even though that child shows no signs of reappearing.)

'I went round to what I continue to think of as Tirpitzstraße 49, about half-past six that evening. The weather had been perfect the whole day, but late afternoon brought an extra perfection. The shadows lengthened, the gardens became more fragrant, a very slight breeze stirred the trees; there was an almost tangible gentleness now to soften all this midsummer exuberance.

'I rang the bell of the house we lived in. It was answered by a man of much the same age as myself. (Later I was to find out that he and I were born the same month of the same year.) His neighbour had not told him of my visit that morning, so I had to explain myself again – this time to an evidently pleased and interested audience. He'd always heard that British people had lived in this house, he said, and now he was very pleased to meet one of them. Could he not offer me some good German beer? I could meet his wife and his children.

'I passed into that house as if I had been living there always. It was not just familiar; it was, I felt, my real home. Not a feature had escaped my powers of preservation: there was my father's study, here was the dining-room where I'd refused to eat so many meals, there was the *Wintergarten* where Debs had slept among the basket furniture. By the drawing-room window, overlooking the terrace where Hannelore had played with her skipping-rope and taught me German songs, we sat, this exact German contemporary of mine, his pretty wife and I, and drank beer and compared our lives. His family – like his wife's – had come from eastern Germany, had chosen Essen because of having connections there, and had lived in an encampment for a while. But soon they'd moved into a better house. Both he and Jutta, his wife, confessed to having to have to make an effort to remember how it all had been. He had trained in Essen to be the dental surgeon he now was, with a very large practice. He had every reason today, therefore, to feel he belonged to Essen, the Essen that had appeared after the war and grown to be a progressive and lively city (though in North Essen there was worse unemployment nowadays than there'd ever been).

'It was different, he said, for people like Frau Schwarz, their neighbour. Her husband had been an official in the Nazi party; everything had been set up for them to have what they thought of as a good life. Even now she remembers the war and the years immediately after it with much bitterness. These last years she'd interested herself principally in what she still called German South-West Africa, belonging to a small circle of women who raise funds for descendants of the original German administration.

'I was taken upstairs. In the room I'd had – when I was you, if I might dare to put it that way – a boy of five years old, their son, was sleeping. In the adjoining room – the room first of all of Finette and Achim, then of my (our) brother – was their baby, a little girl of eleven months.

'I saw the rooms where Toni and Trude and Ursula had slept. I went into the kitchen. I walked all over the garden. I went down into the basement, converted into a flat for a cousin. They were surprised at the accuracy of my memory, how I anticipated aspects of the house before I saw them. I was no longer surprised. Had I not always known the significance of this place to me?

'The evening satisfied, not because it was a dramatic reconciliation with the past, but because it was imbued with the natural pleasure that people should take in meeting others, especially those with whom there is some shared experience.

It was indeed *un*dramatic, far removed from the terrible rain of bombs, all the rhetoric and twisted idealism that had brought them down.

'There was no need even to talk about that. We all three of us knew about it, that we had played no part in it, nor could ever envisage giving consent to any repetition of it, anywhere . . .

'And now I come to when I felt almost in need of seeing you. When I said goodbye to my hosts (and we'd exchanged addresses), I automatically took the direction opposite to that from which I'd come. The road curved round – the bend that had taken St Martin and his retinue away from me – and I walked towards a bank of woodland. I walked in a spirit of great contentment, which increased the further I went. Presently woods enveloped me; I followed a path drenched in the green light of the waning sun filtered through tangles of leaves.

'I happened upon it just before remembering it was there – that abandoned menagerie whose railings kept in not captured animals but a riot of bushes. That sense of an immanence that *you* knew there *I* knew then. And I was glad that you were you, that you'd loved peaceful things, had loathed any evidence of man's ability to destroy, and that you'd extended this love of harmony to the creature-world.

'Why, I wonder, if you're capable of making appearances, didn't you appear to me then? I'd have liked it! It would have been an appropriate ending to a day which is still for me one of the most joyous of my life.'

*

His friends greet him with some excitement. News has come from Romania. This first Christmas of theirs for over three decades has been marked by an event that will divide this day even more sharply from its precursors. The Ceauşescus have been killed. Caught the day before, they have been given summary trial and executed. Macbeth and his Lady, the 'butcher' and his 'hell-kite' are no more. Romanians cannot quite believe it. Has it really happened? Or are they the dupes of their own wishes? No – a film has been taken of the end of the pair, and it will be released tomorrow.

Thus the whole world is made to feel that a suitable last act has taken place; that hubris has received the punishment inherent in itself, that order is slowly being established after the chaos of bloody tragedy. All can know catharsis accordingly. Certainly it is not only Romanians who are incredulous, though their incredulity is obviously of a different complexion from that of members of other societies. Now, with this extraordinary news, everyone has to face the lifting of the Iron Curtain from Europe, to recognise that a new situation and a new era are beginning for history to stamp with the date 1990.

That night the traveller dreams he's back in one of the cells of Prinz-Albrecht-Straße 8. He stands in it bemused, for its walls echo with the rustlings, scrabblings, barkings, whinings of many animals, but he cannot see any of them. Then he notices that the cell-window is open. He's not a prisoner after all; it won't be difficult to climb out. He begins to do so, then wonders if it is wise, with so many beasts audible.

(For if they're not inside, they must be close at hand without.) But since when has he ever feared animals? He calls out to a small boy he can (*just!*) glimpse, but to no avail. He hasn't been heard.

He is just raising himself up on the window-ledge, about to peer over the wall into whatever space the darkness hides, when he wakes up.

# Four

The traveller's friends leave Berlin; some time ago they'd booked an Italian holiday. By himself again – his normal condition! – he dedicates himself to exploration of the city, from the Turkish quarters of the Kreuzberg to the museums of Dahlem, from the bars off the Nollendorfplatz to the Grunewald forest – preserved, not, as once, for princes and their companions, but for the benefit of modern, heterogeneous city-dwellers. But most of all he gives his attention to the Wall which may soon (*Mauer zu verkaufen*) be received by history, standing only in memories.

Twenty-two years ago, he had been taken to Bernauerstraße in the French sector, the most closely guarded area of the Wall, and had upbraided himself, and all others in sight, for consenting to this accommodation of the tourists' appetites . . . Blithely visitors mounted ladders to platforms (many of them are there still) to gaze into the no man's land that introduced East Germany to you. Look-out posts punctuated the opposite side of the Wall, and the Vopos (East German military guards) scrutinised those looking at them. Through binoculars, your eyes met those of a man in a look-out post. *You*, whose identity was totally unknown to him, were, for just those moments, the object of his wholly hostile attention. What did he really think of the people who climbed on to platforms to gratify their curiosity? Was it what he detected as their fundamental imaginative tourism that aroused in him such implacable and visible opposition?

And now, twenty-two years on, and most of the East German sentry stations – even on Bernauerstraße – have gone. Where ruined buildings gauntly stood blocks of flats have gone up, and you would be hard put to it to say, given a photograph of them, to which of the two Berlins any one of these belongs. (In fact, the traveller notes, the East German side contains – surprisingly – more blocks built in a rather traditional German style than does the West.)

Those living in apartments here, one of the least 'desirable' areas of the city, will in the very near future be the residents of the wide avenue that brings the two Berlins together, development on the one side having paralleled development on the other. How long before they can be true neighbours? Wishes and attitudes won't divide them, and a wall no longer will. But the past, the recent past, all its demands and difficulties – that must continue to separate Easterners from Westerners, not indelibly, but maybe enough. As the traveller knows only too well from his own life, the past does not go away leaving nothing behind. The Wall may be pulled down, and the process last only a matter of days, but what it has done to people will not prove so removable.

Bernauerstraße swings into Gartenstraße. At the corner there's a statue of two bears making love, and the traveller, looking at it this cold morning, remembers watching two polar bears doing this in their distressingly small compound in London Zoo. He'd been deeply moved by the extraordinary and protracted tenderness the bears showed to one another, their lickings, caresses, grunts of appreciation and desire. He'd wondered anew at the wilful blindness of humans, who've denied to animals capacities for passion and altruism. That last wall . . .

As he's thinking this, he hears a noise of which there can be only one source. Someone is firing a gun. But maybe he himself has conjured it out of the depressing surroundings – the Wall at its grimmest, flat blocks at their most jerry-built and inhospitable. But no, there it sounds again!

The street is quite deserted – even of cars. The traveller looks ahead of him, and sees, high up on the balcony, a man (features blurred; sleet is lightly falling) standing with a rifle in his hands. He is firing straight ahead of him at the Wall.

For a moment fear and astonishment freeze the traveller. More shots ring out, and he is as motionless as the stone bears. Then he pulls himself together, turns round, moves carefully (for it may not be out of the question for the armed man to turn round, and aim elsewhere) and walks (very quickly) down Bernauerstraße again. He recalls having passed a hospice, and so calls there to inform the porter of what he's just seen. The porter rings the police, who appear within ten minutes in a green armour-plated van, and ask the traveller to accompany them to the place where he'd seen and heard the man. Of course he is no longer there. 'Was he shooting at the Wall?' asks one of the policemen. 'Yes, it seemed to me that he was,' says the traveller. 'It happens,' says the policeman, smiling rather wryly. 'It happens more often than you might think.'

The Wall itself is insane, the fruit of paranoia. Therefore it is fitting that it should engender insane paranoia in others. And if the traveller had died as a result of this unknown, unfindable man (and he may, of course, have been firing blanks!) that too would have had a horrible aptness. No one has the right to think himself only a tourist where the Berlin Wall is concerned, even in the terminal stages of its existence.

He stands beside the memorial to its last fatal casualty – the end of a row of commemorations just beyond the Reichstag.

CHRIS GUEFFROY

† 6.2.89. (20 Jahre)

Ein Berliner

The carnations placed below the tribute are still fresh. He died this year, in February! – so recently that it wouldn't be at all difficult to work out what he himself had been doing on the day of this youth's death. And at twenty years of age! It seems to the traveller that at twenty he'd known, done, even thought so dreadfully little that he'd hardly experienced existence.

'*Opfer der Honecker Diktatur*,' (Victim of the Honecker dictatorship) his friends proclaimed, and:

> *Wir saßen im Gefangnis.*
> *Du hast Dein Leben gegeben.*

*Wir werden Dich* nie *vergessen!*
– Steffi und Sylvana


(We were sitting in prison. You've given your life. We will *never* forget you!)

It seems tragically apt that this final victim should have been so young. If he'd waited only a matter of months he could have walked over the border, to the accompaniment of smiles, and gone to collect *Begrüßungsgeld*. The dedicated lover of freedom must always be impatient!

His killers would doubtless have justified themselves ideologically. It's an ideology that has dismantled itself as easily as it dismantled its greatest monument. And no people seem happier about it than these Christmas-season Vopos – smiling away amicably as if arrests and shootings existed only inside the visitors' heads.

And, of course, this may be exactly how they regard their own situation now – erstwhile reluctant state servants who at last can seem as they truly are!

Two more slogans from the Wall. In Bernauerstraße:


IST BRÜDERLICHKEIT UTOPISCH?


(Is fraternity Utopian?) Who can answer this? At Checkpoint Charlie:


CHARLIE'S RETIRED.


Well, that *does* seem to be true – at least for the time being!

\*

The child still fails to reappear. But the traveller is occupied with real, flesh-and-blood encounters. A German friend who's written a study of the great Berlin novelist Alfred Döblin has arrived in the city; they spend much time together in both the West and the East. He reaffirms the contacts he made with those protesters on behalf of the animals, *die Tierversuchsgegner*. In the Haus am Checkpoint Charlie, with it moving collection of photographs and relics of Wall-defiers and victims, he spends many hours; exhibited are paintings by young Berliners, of the Wall as they apprehend it. He is struck by the profusion of animal imagery, the cornered rats, the imprisoned birds.

New Year's Eve approaches. People anticipate it in their talk, are excited by the prospect of it, and also dread it a little. Perhaps it'll be an anti-climax? Perhaps it will be an occasion primarily for worry – or even distress? No one can quite be sure what these strange days have unleashed, what concomitants hope and elation have.

Over a quarter of a million visitors arrive in Berlin. The major avenues prepare themselves for the celebrations; trim green caravans appear on the Straße des 17 Juni and elsewhere, lavatories for the host.

The weather gets intensely cold, an icy mist hanging over woods and canals.

The traveller sees, once or twice in the crowds, a man he thinks resembles his father. His father would have been

**207**

pleased by this *trompe l'oeil*; he always liked to think he looked German. A few hours before midnight on 31 December the telephone rings in the Wilmersdorf apartment; it is the traveller's oldest friend, from England, giving him good wishes. He too is part-German.


The air smells of gunpowder, and from all directions come the loud retorts of exploding fireworks. Youths throw crackers on the pavements, among pedestrians, down the maws of underground stations, into bars. Indeed the firecrackers become – within half an hour or so – a sort of species of insect that has descended on Berlin, noisy, maybe dangerous, but quite unavoidable. They even appear, somewhat to general alarm, in the congested interiors of the U-Bahn trains, gliding forwards to a new point in time.

If one had been dropped, a complete stranger to Berlin, in any part of the Tiergarten, on any stretch of the Wall from Bernauerstraße all the way to Prinzenstraße, one would surely end up before the Brandenburger Tor, simply because everyone to be seen is making their way there. It's like joining some ubiquitous quest; each bend or junction of the paths and roads brings yet more hurrying people – people of all kinds – into view. The crackers jump alongside them, as though to spur them on.


The traveller left his flat at twenty-past ten. By eleven o'clock he has entered the Straße des 17 Juni. The many scurrying bands he's followed are, at a turn of the feet, a blink of the eye, absorbed into the multitude before the gate; it's the ocean receiving the streams and rivers that flow into it. And just as an ocean is made up of the same element as contributes to it yet is other, is its own irrefutable self, so does the mass now appear before him; people form it, yet it is more than people – it is identifiable also as an expression of their wills, and every person who approaches it does so knowing this, honouring the fact. You pass into it to be changed – and, if in some cases a little fearfully, all do so gladly.

Later he is to learn that between three and four hundred thousand people gathered to see in the New Year by the Brandenburger Tor. But standing in the crowd, carefully edging to a position quite close to the gate, he finds it impossible to make any assessment of numbers, just as the minutes inexorably dying towards the moment of midnight 1989–1990 have become unsusceptible to measurement, as if the multitude here had scooped up time and held it in their united breaths until all were ready to declare the new year begun.

People are standing in tiered rows upon the Wall; people are even on top of the Brandenburger Tor itself, astride the Quadriga; people are thrown by the city and what it is experiencing into relief against the dark sky, and even the zooming brilliance of firework displays does not diminish their stature. *Wir sind das Volk!* But this is not just a celebration of Germany – and of a German resolution of difficulties . . . For perhaps the first time in his whole life the traveller forgets that dialogue between Britain and Germany which has so governed his life. Neither claims his allegiance; his allegiance is elsewhere, is here, among the tens of thousands whose one desire is to witness the happiness of others.

The moment when the 1980s end and a new and freer decade begins happens – like all great events – in a wholly unexpected way. The traveller has arrived here at this nerve-centre of Europe, at this present kissing-gate between East and West, prepared for almost anything except what in fact occurs. He is prepared for displays of emotion, for shouts and songs, for hysterical cries, for wild laughter and for tears, for some ugliness, for jubilation.

But the massing here is an expression of something so profoundly important within each person present – and also within the millions who physically are not – that the antici-pated moment of passage occurs in solemn quiet. It is rever-ence that is palpable, reverence for each other. So the pop-ping of champagne-corks and the explosion of yet more fireworks occur some minutes *after* 1990 has begun.

About four o'clock the traveller gets into bed in the Wil-mersdorf apartment. To have this dream:

He is leaving Berlin, has boarded the train at Zoo Station to be taken through the East German forest. But where to? Not back to England, it would seem, for there is no sign of the frontier (though that could have been dismantled), and no indications that they are to pass through Braunschweig, the first city of West Germany for the England-bound express.

He is alighting at a nondescript sort of place – suggesting in its neutral architecture no particular country. Here are emporia with plate-glass windows, banks, characterless bars, pedestrian precincts. A lot of people are about; it's a summer evening. How quickly a year passes!

Moving in the crowd just a matter of yards in front of him, lithe, dark-haired, brightly dressed, is someone he has been searching for all his life. It is Finette's Achim – whose face has escaped him all these years. But when he turns his head, he will see, he knows, Rembrandt's David who played to Saul, the David modelled on Jewish boys from the Amsterdam ghetto. He knows this because his mother had once remarked on the uncanny resemblance.

Achim doesn't turn round, however. The traveller moves forward more quickly. Now a truth has been borne upon him. He's been unable to bring Achim's features to mind not because he hated him or resented him, but because he loved him. Loved him so much that when he passed out of his life, his mind refused to accept the grief and blanked out its source.

The traveller breaks into a run. His quarry gets no nearer. By the time he surfaces, sweating, into the tangible world, he knows that he never would have caught up with him. It doesn't matter now that he hasn't. He's identified the love-object of his early German life, and the object of his private search ever since. Berlin has shown him a truth about himself after all.


Morning brings news of a fatality during the festivities of the night. A television stand collapsed: one dead, and a number seriously injured. Happy times do not deliver us into safety. Only at one's stupidest does one deceive oneself into thinking that they do. But the nature of a death transfigures it, even – one dares to suppose – for the person whose experience it is. It is better to die in a joyful crowd than by the guns of the Vopos, like poor Chris Gueffroy.

It's snowing in the city now. Prospects tease the eye, presenting themselves one minute, being engulfed in snowflakes the next. The streets are exceedingly, unbelievably quiet – for most Berliners are sleeping – and the snow muffles what traffic and movement there is. With the efficiency that tradition and cliché – and truthful reporting also – ascribe to Germans, the pavements and roadways, so profuse with litter, spent fireworks, broken bottles and smashed glasses in the small hours (slowing down the homeward walker) are almost clean now. Where not, machines looking like prehistoric monsters are at work, silently scooping up rubbish.

By the time he has reached the site of yesterday's celebrations the snow is coming down so hard that it's difficult to look straight ahead. The Brandenburger Tor, strangely white through the whiteness of the falling flakes, becomes difficult to hold in view. Just like the future itself, the traveller thinks. We rejoice, and we're right to rejoice, but we know the problems ahead and know the ineptitude of most of us who make up a jubilant mass when confronting any one of them. How can economic union be effected between the Germanies? Won't the present influx of East Germans into West Germany bring the DDR close to fiscal collapse? What do the politicians of the rest of the world really want as regards *Einheit*? Will East Germans decide that what they want above all else is a society based on humane principles, opposed to war and to any crude nationalism, and determined to play a part in the amelioration of the human and natural worlds? Or will they listen to quite other voices, issued to them via the machinery of cunning neighbours? What will happen to the respective commitments to NATO and the Warsaw Pact? Will these organisations become obsolete, history-book names only, within but a short time?

The snow keeps tumbling down.

The traveller feels a tweak at his elbow. He looks round. And sees – as he'd thought, as he'd hoped – that small boy who'd appeared to him in the former Prinz-Albrecht-Straße.

'Why weren't you there yesterday?' he says. 'It was wonderful. I'd have liked your company.'

'You didn't need me,' says the child.

'I suppose I didn't need you in Essen either,' says the traveller a little churlishly, 'when I revisited *your* home!'

'No,' said the child, 'you didn't need me there, either. Happiness such as you knew then doesn't require the services of someone like myself.'

'And now does, I suppose,' says the traveller sarcastically. He now can see written on the mighty plinth of the arch the words: VIVE L'ANARCHIE! Well, there could be worse wishes.

'You remember how I was,' the child is continuing. 'I wouldn't be satisfied with invitations, commands, to enjoy myself. To surrender my doubts and hopes in the name of some general ease. "It was all so wonderful," you say, and I'm sure you're right. As you've reminded me, I wasn't there. But more wonderful still could be what we go on, resolutely,

213

to create from it, what we refuse to let happen, knowing the lessons yesterday, and what went to its making, have taught us. One wall is down – or virtually so. But other walls remain; the wall between the prosperous nations and the poorer ones, the wall between man and the animals. Europe is in danger now of becoming so satiated with self-satisfaction and self-concern – yes, even on account of this East–West *rapprochement* – that it forgets the far more numerous who share our world with us.

'I imagine you haven't forgotten that Martinmas carol you used to hear in Essen every November. It's rather appropriate weather to remember it in:

> *Sankt Martin ritt durch Schnee und Wind*
> *sein Roß, das trug ihn fort geschwind.*
> *Sankt Martin ritt mit leichtem Mut:*
> *sein Mantel deckt' ihn warm und gut.*
>
> *Im Schnee, da saß ein armer Mann,*
> *hatt' Kleider nicht, hatt' Lumpen an.*
> *O helft mir doch in meiner Not*
> *sonst ist der bittre Frost mein Tod!*
>
> *Sankt Martin zog die Zügel an,*
> *sein Roß stand still beim armen Mann,*
> *Sankt Martin mit dem Schwerte teilt'*
> *den warmen Mantel unverweilt.*
>
> *Sankt Martin gab den halben still,*
> *der Bettler rasch ihm danken will.*
> *Sankt Martin aber ritt in Eil'*
> *hinweg mit seinem Mantelteil.*

(St Martin rode through snow and wind/his horse carried him along quickly./St Martin rode with a light heart:/his cloak wrapped him warm and well./In the snow there sat a poor man,/he hadn't any clothes on, he had only tatters./O help me in my need,/or else the bitter frost is my death!/St Martin pulled on the reins,/his horse stopped still by the poor man,/St Martin with a sword cut/the warm cloak unhesitatingly./St Martin gave one half quietly,/the beggar wants to thank him./But St Martin rode off in a hurry,/rode away with his portion of the cloak.)

'I don't think we've got to agree with St Martin on matters of dogma to find him an example for us all. He was a peace-lover – refusing, incidentally, to serve as a soldier – because he loved fellow-beings as he loved himself. The sight of another's suffering was intolerable to him; he did all he could.

'That wouldn't be an epitaph for many of us.

'We shouldn't do good things out of some duty, but because we are only truly happy when we're all equal and the walls are down. These days have shown that. So let's keep St Martin in mind, we prosperous Europeans, and follow him like those children in Tirpitzstraße – sharing with all others, down to the most unimportant-seeming members of the creature-world.'

Fiercer and fiercer fly the flakes. For a moment the traveller is transported in his mind back to Bredeney, to all those bright and many-shaped lanterns held up stoutly against the dark. We should be able to see all our acts thus, he thinks.

He swings round to reply to the child, but, like the Brand-enburger Tor itself these last moments, he has vanished.

# Afterword

*St Martin's Ride* closes with New Year's Day, 1990, a day of uncertain forward-looking. Now, two years later, I am asked to write an afterword for the paperback edition. 1992 is the year that had been generally billed as the 'European' one, which would see further and definitive moves towards European — that is, Western European — unity, not to say union. But now — New Year's Day, 1992 — it seems as though, after an Edinburgh Conference this coming December, it will be *1993* that will be the 'European' year.

What one means by Europe now is not what one meant when 1990 opened. Germany, after forty-five years, is one country again, and for all the social and economic difficulties it is undergoing, unification already seems to have taken place a long time ago. Poland, Hungary, Czechoslovakia, with their democratically elected non-Communist governments, stand poised for admission into the European community. Famously neutral Sweden no longer holds back from the EC; its new right-wing coalition government is intent on undoing the famous 'Swedish model', and gearing the economy for competitive entry. The imposed eccentricity of Finland and Austria are

217

relevant no more. Above all there has been, after dramatic events in which the whole Western world vicariously participated, the dissolution of the Soviet Union. It was finally announced on Christmas Day, 1991, in Gorbachev's resignation speech. Russia has taken the Soviet Union's vacant seat at the UN but out of the former Union we have other determinedly European nations: Ukraine, Byelorussia, Moldavia. While, some months ago, the Baltic states of Estonia, Latvia, and Lithuania, whose sovereignty went under in the power-struggle between Hitler's Germany and Stalin's Russia, regained independence, international recognition, and membership of the United Nations.

Meanwhile, in what, in my early years, was held up as the great exception to the rule of Eastern Europe, that every Communist country was a ruthlessly maintained Soviet satellite — we have chaos: Yugoslavia is in the grip of a savage civil war. Slovenia and Croatia have already declared independence, which has been limitedly ackowledged elsewhere; Croatia has provoked widespread reprisals from the predominantly Serbian Yugoslav Federal Army. Perhaps in our Titoist apostrophes we failed to do justice to the precarious nature of this unionof six diverse republics. Cities that have been tangible metaphors for Western culture in an Eastern European context — for example, the jewel of the Adriatic, Dubrovnik — have been bombed and shelled, their inhabitants terrorised and killed. Now there is unrest and fear in Bosnia–Herzegovina, that nerve-centre which saw the opening shot of the first great War.

Truly, to our surprise, we stand far closer to an earlier Europe — perhaps even the pre-Sarajevo one — than to the Cold War continent in which we have grown up. For most

Western Europeans, and the British in particular, the Second World War's aftermath had taken on an indelible colour. At times it can seem that that Meiklejohn atlas which annoyed the small boy in *St Martin's Ride* by not reflecting what the Second World War had brought about could almost be back in date. Certainly we now have the fullest map of Europe to live with of my lifetime, a very populous one indeed, bristling with the demands of peoples kept in some kind of limbo for half a century, and in many cases, longer still, the nature of whose existence was blurred by simplistic cartography. The bloody crack-up of Yugoslavia, the already savage civil war in Georgia, with President Gamsakhordia incarcerated, these remind us that Slovenes, Croats, Albanians, Georgians, have lively identities and historical memories which imposed political systems have finally proved impotent to disguise. Not that we should direct critical attack solely on to these systems. We should direct it on to ourselves as well — we who have allowed fifty years of rhetoric and anti-Communist propaganda to keep us fearfully and culpably ignorant of the complexities of countries and peoples. Latterly they have burst upon our consciousness like those sleeping hidden armies from a mountain in Eastern European folklore.

The paradox of 1990s Europe is that Eastern Europe, in emancipating itself from union and affiliation, has looked to the Western European nations as exempla, while they are seeking to bind themselves more closely to one another, to attain union as never before. Now the countries of the dissolved Soviet Union weigh Commonwealth and National liberties against each other. Within this situation apparent inconsistencies (that are, on a deeper level, consistencies) abound. For instance Britain is the most articulately reluctant country with respect to unity, the most apt to cite its ancient sovereign traditions. Germany is a comparatively enthusiastic integrationist. Yet it is Germany not Britain who has tried to insist on Croation independence from the Yugoslav federation. German – and indeed much general European – willingness to participate in Yugoslavia contrasts with British denunciation of the desirability of armed involvement there. Yet, only months before, in the terrible Gulf War, Britain lost no opportunity for decrying its European allies for (as they saw it) lack of commitment. 'We Won't Die for Yugoslavia' has been proudly headlined as Major's declaration on the recent matter; but during the Gulf War young Germans registering themselves as conscientious objectors were jeered at in another headline as 'The Shame of Germany'. No question of 'We Won't Die for Kuwait'!

Indeed a pattern already exists that Britain will differ from Europe more often than not, that spiritually it confronts both the new and old, and yet still evolving, map of Europe rather as it confronts it geographically, from a detached position and at an angle.

One has, I think, to admit that this enlargement of Europe, this proliferation of national voices, in significant ways vitiates the idea of Europe, or rather of the EC, that was for so long fostered, and to which British people had, and with much difficulty, to educate themselves after 1950.


For someone of my age it is almost impossible to dissociate the Community from the original Six, and from the attempt which that banding together represented a healing, through commerce, of the cruel differences between France and Germany. Viewed, as we growing British had to view the 'EEC' of then, at a distance, from the outside, it seemed an overwhelmingly foreign (or unBritish) amalgam of republicanism and enlightened or secularized Catholicism – for all that the Benelux countries are monarchies, and that over half the Netherlands and 49 per cent of West Germany is Protestant. Inevitably experiences from my past confirm that sad sense of an enterprise quite separate from British concerns.

The small boy of Part One of *St Martin's Ride* returned to an England soon to hail a new Queen with the now fantastic-seeming pageantry of the 1953 Coronation. This all but gave a literal meaning to the words: 'Thine is the Kingdom, the Power, and the Glory'. All Britain – and beyond it the Commonwealth – was mobilised to do homage to the country's unique, hallowed nature. The Queen was, after all, also head of the Church of England; she was enthroned in the Abbey as no ordinary being, but rather as an anointed special creature of destiny. Nor was she sovereign of one country among others. A history apart was consecrated afresh that day, and the consecration had special importance for being so near in time to the dreadful events of the War. I remember, as a boy living in the north of England, being brought to London (for the first time) to see the city decorated for the Coronation, great arches over the streets, everywhere symbolic flowers and crowns, solemn and impressive testimony to Britain's noble difference from all other nations. Something of this impression of London has never forsaken me; its Coronation splendour can hang over it for me still. Most children who gaped at all this knew the vision of Britain that lay behind it from history lessons and books. Perhaps, if they belonged to the middle class as I did, they learnt it from my own favourites *Our Island Story* and *Our Empire Story* by H. E. Marshall, or from the same author's *English Literature for Girls and Boys* which presented all writers as a sort of conscious cavalcade of British patriots, from properly Anglo-Saxon Bede and Caedmon to Chaucer, Spenser, Shakespeare, and the translators who worked on King James' Bible, which made of Hebrew and Greek scriptures something peculiarly, wonderfully, indissolubly English. (Some of this aspect of the Coronation Year is caught in A. S. Byatt's fine novel, *The Virgin in the Garden*, where a great deal is made – hence the title – of the new Queen being a second Elizabeth about to usher in a new age.) Not much room for thoughts about Europe here, let alone about what the War, only eight years over, had really meant for the participant countries. The pomp was to transfigure everything, and indeed the Coronation still seems to be one of the very few post-War events in which all Britons equally shared, which cut across the tragically pervasive barriers of social class.

Not that the War was forgotten. Quite the contrary!

It is impossible to exaggerate the sentimental reverence, both individually and collectively, that came over British people at this time, when they spoke of how it all was during the War years. To remember my boyhood is at once to remember interminable hours of hearing my parents' contemporaries extolling British behaviour then. What the British went through (we don't use the word 'suffer' – the British are too plucky to suffer!) was altogether different from what other

222

peoples had gone through, because the virtue of the British had been proved by their not being contaminated by having Germans on their soil. (Nothing was known, it would seem, about the Channel Islands.) The retrospective love-affair with the War in which the whole country indulged itself centred on the British at home – not, for example, on the fighting in the desert or in Italy – where attempts to undermine and invade were valiantly resisted and the status quo was preserved, thanks largely to humour, common sense, and pluck. It seems hardly fanciful to see all this as a metaphor in truth for another kind of isolation – from European renewal and forward-thinking. Undoubtedly its vocabulary was to resurface with Mrs Thatcher – cf. the terms of Sir Geoffrey Howe's seminal resignation speech of November 1990. The Coronation confer-red not just respectability but divine approval on an intensify-ing isolationism.

Republicanism and Catholicism are twinned in the British mind because in their own country the monarchy is inseparable from Protestantism and a state Protestant Church. I think too little – at any rate in popular discussion – has been made of this when considering our relationship with Europe. I believe that a hidden distrust/fear/dislike of Catholicism underpins our unease about Europe, fuelling such as Mrs Thatcher herself. Given our education it would not be very surprising; breaking away from the Pope has been presented to successive gener-ations as at once marking purity in national identity and an-other kind of purity, in religious vision and practice. To make my earlier point in reverse, of the original Six countries, Belgium, Italy, and Luxemburg are indelibly Catholic, anti-clerical France is nevertheless inseparable from Catholicism, and, at the time of writing, the Netherlands and Germany have basically Catholic administrations. Of the later arrivals the Catholicism of Spain, Portugal, and Ireland scarcely needs to be commented on, and Greece belongs to the Orthodox community of Churches. Only Denmark is a Protestant monarchy like Britain, and it can hardly be coincidence that Denmark is perhaps, after Britain, the most notably unenthusiastic about a 'federalised' Europe.

Having a Protestant state Church (with a long history of vernacular liturgy) means that the society does not look outside its own frontiers, political, cultural, and linguistic, for guidance or reverence, in the way that all Catholic societies have perforce to look to Rome. Concepts of national virtue thus get inextricably entangled with those of religious excellence. Even today — as a very occasional visitor — I am strongly struck by how much an Anglican service is a way of worshipping some inherited Platonic England. Architecture, music, language, practices are all a way of keeping in touch with an England that social upheaval has shattered: standing underneath the great pillars or listening to the bells we remember, as we rarely otherwise do, the medieval past. Readings from the Bible and the singing of psalms lead us back to the Renaissance, Shakespeare, and the beginnings of national glory, the later manifestations of which will be paid tribute to in the hymns, so many of them Victorian, where imagery about God derives from the British Empire. (And one has to add that Christian orthodoxy encourages thinking of God as King and Father, and Christ as Prince and Son, hence my own picture of the *König* of the *Kasperltheater* as God. This, of course, compounds the fusion.)

In the months that have passed since finishing *St Martin's Ride*, months in which the traveller of the book's second part has tried to unlearn his travelling habits, and to settle down to British life again, the national reservations about Europe and European unity have been matters of major concern, and it is difficult to see how this will not be the central British preoccupation of the Nineties. A newly returned traveller can feel he is confronting a curious and disturbing phenomenon.

All proposals for a closer-knit unity of currency, foreign policy, defence, and social legislation are greeted by Britain with such intense emotional reaction that one could come very near to believing – as one fears many must – that the plans have been made with the express intention of undermining Britain out of all other nations, of deliberately and perversely setting out to undo ancient British traditions and ways. Mention is very rarely made of other countries' response to these proposals or to the fact that in no other country do they engender such extraordinary agitation. Indeed one might think they are never debated elsewhere, have meaning solely for Britain. But the traveller knows that French, Dutch, Italians, Germans, and Spanish do not react to plans for further integration as though they had been singled out for malicious attack, and, furthermore, from conversations with members of different groups within these European societies, that many feel – on the contrary – excited and stimulated by the changes put forward. They talk of a new multinational community, one that draws on what nations near to each other both geographically and in terms of historical development share, and which, through common laws and policies and markets, eschews what made them enter into conflict.

Not so the British, from whom — especially in their un-democratically owned press — enthusiasm for any kind of integration would appear to be seen as capitulation, anti-patriotism, and — in my terminology — blasphemy. Think of all the fervid manifestations of suspicion these last two years have seen. Here I can only itemise a few: Delors' views on the merits of currency union earned 'Up Yours, Delors' from the country's biggest-circulation daily, plus its devoting column after column of anti-French remarks, including jokes ridiculing them for their defeats in the last War. But this wasn't enough for the *Sun*, who went on to organise a whole nation-wide anti-French day with rallying posts where Britons could deliver themselves of anti-French pronouncements and gestures. It has to be said that this obscene 'event' was a flop, but nevertheless it drew no words of complaint from those in power; indeed Mrs Thatcher and Kenneth Baker were sufficiently admiring of the *Sun* to send it fulsome congratulations on its twenty-first birthday, a '*Sun*-reader named Ken' publicly and complacently declaring that 'when he wanted some views/ and some up-to-date news/ he gave the *Sun* ten out of ten'. While many European politicians suffered under and courageously resisted Nazi Germans in the War, it was left to a *British* politician (Nicholas Ridley) in the emotional days leading up to German unity to insult the people with unnecessary and totally contextless allusions to Hitler. He was not seriously rebuked; Mrs Thatcher implied rather that he was a martyr. Not so long after this came her own histrionic and, in the event, historically significant outburst of anti-Europeanism, brought about by her un-preparedness for Andreotti's conference manoeuvres. But here, of course, the story alters, since undoubtedly her 'No! No! No!'

226

was, to a very considerable extent responsible for her departure from office. And Mrs Thatcher's downfall it increasingly seems legitimate to view was a concession by the British that there are forms of overt belligerence to the Community that they themselves of their own volition joined which are mistaken, inappropriate, and self-destructive. And, of course, a highly significant section of the British community does think this. Oddly, one might say perversely, this section has to behave very cautiously, to be restrained in its advocacies, and, oddly and perversely too, to be ever-mindful of the press's peculiar appetite for opportunities for xenophobic effusions.

Thus, after Mrs Thatcher's demise, we have had the French qualifications about participation in the Gulf War treated as if the professional French forces had suddenly been seized with an attack of nerves, of the gutlessness which the British, despite so much empirical evidence to the opposite, have decided is a mark of being French; hence another shrill and vicious tabloid headline, 'Where the **** are the French?' The French in fact proceeded to play a determining part in the War; this was not widely reported, however. Also the Germans, popularly viewed just before Unification as Huns waiting in the wings to begin aggressive take-overs of other countries, were (as has been mentioned) lambasted for cowardice, for sticking to the very terms of non-combative international action that Britain had previously been so insistent on. Cowardice was also found present in the Belgians and the Spanish.

The culmination of so much xenophobic activity was of course the three days of the Maastricht Conference, December 1991. Not the least extraordinary feature of British approaches to Maastricht was the intense media coverage, in which the nation was virtually seduced into believing that its disappearance was at stake. Those who had thought that Sir Geoffrey Howe's resignation speech might have marked a turning point in official attitudes and phraseology about Europe were proved wrong, and Mrs Thatcher herself rose phoenix-like to remind people of her convictions. With such popular feeling (apparently) at home, perhaps Mr Major had no alternative to behaving the way he did: for providing safeguards for Britain for the Single Currency Union which almost everybody is sure that Britain will anyway have to accept; and with which, according to the polls, a majority appears to be in sympathy (aside perhaps from its European provenance).

An eminent English writer remarked to me: 'How strange that it has all been consistently presented in the language of war.' The press would have it that Mr Major returned to England as an honourably victorious man who had fought for his country and won through. Particularly resented were French expressions of federal hopes (and doesn't our jokey way of referring to Federalism as 'the "F" word' speak volumes about the state of our national psyche?). So perhaps again the *Sun* provided a good idea of British feeling when it gave as its headline the day the conference ended: 'Major-3, French-0'.

It was salutary and chastening to examine the European papers, to appreciate the full oddity of Britain's antics with respect to the Social Charter in particular. The Italian *Repubblica*, of the right, said it well: '*Europa a undice. Ma Londra guesta la fiesta*, Europe for eleven. But London spoils the party.'

Perhaps we *should* have a referendum. Certainly it is difficult to argue, given the emotional hostility to unity, that the British *should* be forced to submit to an organisation they disapprove of and fear. (One finds oneself succumbing to Eurosceptic terminology, for, in truth, the word 'submit' is quite inapposite.) But perhaps the hostility shouldn't be a 'given', since it has not been entertained in the rational parts of the mind capable of weighing pros and cons. For me British reaction is pathological, and I believe this the more strongly when I contemplate the many and regular fearful acts of aggression by young British people all over the Continent. Acts which if committed by foreigners here would rightly be received with the most passionate and incredulous resentment: a peculiarly memorable instance is the episode last year of boys from Staffordshire on Corfu capturing a smallholder's donkey, blinding it by repeatedly ramming a stake through its eyes, and then killing it.

The pathology derives from that intertwining in the British psyche of God, virtue, Britain (England most of all), traditional hierarchy, and government which I have referred to above. It is spitting against the Holy Ghost to admit the inevitable flaws and limitations of British national inheritance and to think that things are better elsewhere. Nevertheless the British *do* find flaws in their own country and *are* impressed by the countries of others. Interestingly, in a recent American survey of European attitudes, far more British were patriotic in the sense of believing in fighting for their country right or wrong than other Europeans, yet at the same time topped the polls in the wish to leave their country and live elsewhere. The two attitudes could be thought paradoxical if not contradictory. But perhaps they are not. Who really wants to live in a country where it is blasphemy not to want to serve it right or wrong? What comfortable home can there be with such a jealous God, who is invoked at every touch and turn, whether we are dealing with criminal behaviour or coinage, dogs, or the teaching of history?

One motive of mine in writing *St Martin's Ride* was a wish to convey the unusual situation of my early childhood in which the suffering I saw around me could be attributed to my fellow-countrymen while my experiences of human warmth and imaginative peace came from the 'guilty' Germans. This vision has of course been subjected and contexted by later experience and knowledge. Somehow or other I have had to accommodate loved childhood figures into the Third Reich, of which they had once been members, however reluctant. Somehow or other the appalling destruction of German cities carried out by Englishmen had to be placed alongside so much admirable comportment of the British during – and indeed immediately after – the War. I believe such balance as I have achieved in my life owes much to these necessary mental exertions. Therefore I believe that the British – or maybe I should write 'we British' – have to make similar adjustments as we prepare ourselves for the possibility (I put it no more strongly) of deeper membership of the Community we substantially chose to enter. Demands have, after all, been made on other peoples for self-overhaul, the Germans preeminently before being allowed to be a nation again. (See President Richard von Weizsäcker's integration speech!) Demythologising ourselves, secularising ourselves, can do nothing but good. The very hysteria of the anti-Europe voices in Britain convinces me that, whatever my particular reservations (and I have quite a number), to isolate ourselves is to sink further into our already alarming and destructive pathological condition.

Whatever impression *St Martin's Ride* may have given readers, I would like to state here that I am profoundly bound up with my country of Britain, that I am fascinated, inspired, and, at times, made proud by its culture and achievements. I have crossed the Channel many, many times and it is true to say that every time I have done so, I have felt a catch in the heart at the sight of the cliffs of Dover, at the peaceful-seeming, intimate-looking country that you glimpse piled on top of the greensward above those white sea-walls. But I like the idea of this benign-faced Britain *receiving* visitors, offering itself and its ways of life to others, not of it stubbornly, stupidly, and sneeringly barricading itself against most comers, and anyone different.

The British have so much to give to Europe as well as to receive from it — they can give in their attitudes to animals, treatment of plant-life, stimulation of creative work in children, to name domains in which I myself am particularly interested. And I also believe that during the Gulf War something very profound occurred among certain British people that will have repercussions elsewhere. Many of us were moved when we heard British airmen talking before and after their operations. Now we learn that it was their disgust at further killing, at having to carry out strafings and bombings they were far from convinced were necessary, that led to the cessation of hostilities. No one could accuse those airmen of not being brave, of not doing what their government, their country, required, yet there came a point when their hatred of destroying fellow-humans, fellow living-beings, asserted itself above all else, and *that* was the voice they obeyed. Disapproving of, more, detesting the Gulf War though I did, I salute these men with heartfelt emotion. It seems very fitting to conclude this afterword to a book dealing so largely with the effects of bombing with this new and entirely British achievement.

Paul Binding
London October 1991